CH00847026

Pentecost
Expressed

A fresh look at the gifts of the Holy Spirit

Peter Butt

ISBN: 1724567152
ISBN-13: 978-1724567154

DEDICATION

It is 50 years since my wife and I began our journey into ministry. Along the way there have been so many who have impacted our lives. This has shaped who we are and what we are still becoming. Friends, colleagues, partners in ministry, we thank for your contribution – This book is dedicated to you and to our four children, Susanne, Juliet, Frances and Andrew you have been a major part of the story. Thank you all!.

CONTENTS

COMMENDATIONS

John Noble - Chairman of the National Charismatic and Pentecostal Leadership Conference from 1984 – 2006

In his second book of a trilogy Peter is addressing what I consider to be an urgent need in the Western Church. Since the early days of the Charismatic Renewal and the powerful and widespread outpouring of the Holy Spirit, we have neglected to continue encouraging and teaching on the receiving and operation of the gifts. As a result in many churches there is little evidence of supernatural activity.

Here Peter provides us with a well written and balanced guide to the gifts of the Holy Spirit with practical help on how to move forward in their use. It is peppered with both biblical and personal illustrations from his own experience. The book is a must for anyone keen to grow in their understanding and development of life in the Spirit. It is ideal for use in groups with the support of church leadership.

Billy Kennedy - Leader, Pioneer network and Senior Leader, New Community Church, Southampton

This a good read, it is even better than the first one!

Paul Randerson – Senior Leader, Kings Lynn and Breckland Christian Fellowships:

"This second book contains good balanced teaching with great examples which stir us up to carry His presence and gifts into our world. The world so needs to see signs to accompany the words we speak. Well done! This book will be a great resource to leaders too. Thank you for writing this."

Adam Clewer – Leader – New Community Church, Southampton.

"This is good, really good in fact. Your first book was good; this is even better."

Basil D'Souza - Leader of International Christian Leadership Network and Covenant Blessings Church, Mumbai, India.

Peter has done it again with this latest 'gift' wrapped as a book – Pentecost Expressed… With his engaging style, clear teaching and hands-on practicum, Peter inspires and challenges one to explore, discover and experience what the baptism in the Holy Spirit can do for every person. His lucid manner opens the door to understanding and operating in the gifts.

A must-read brilliant hand-book of a gift for those who yearn a strong biblical foundation, earnestly desire the gifts and passionately long for a demonstration of the dunamis power of the Holy Spirit. An outflow from a sharply anointed man I am privileged to have had a ringside view of for over two decades.

Ian Green, Executive Director of Ian Green Communications
www.iangreen.org

Peter, has done an outstanding job practically and theologically explaining and illustrating the work of the Spirit. Some of his insights will be new to some historic Pentecostals, and fresh thinking for those born into the charismatic movement. He gives some outstanding and thoughtful exposition of scriptures that have been confusing to some. With 50 years of Christian Leadership experience his practical application of the work of the Spirit is inspirational and liberating. For those who hunger for more of the Spirit, this volume inspires the heart, and guides the mind to that hunger being satisfied.

INTRODUCTION

In my previous book "Pentecost Now... Pentecost Then...", I looked at the importance of a personal encounter with the Holy Spirit, a personal baptism in the Holy Spirit and an on-going walk with the Holy Spirit. In this book we will see how the Holy Spirit impacted the lives of people and caused the church in its early days to grow exponentially both in quantity and quality. The place of the "gifts of the Spirit" and the "ministry gifts of Christ" are important and significant, in that early church explosion of life and growth we read of in the book of Acts. This book is intending to highlight one of these issues.

Another book will follow, looking at apostolic leadership. It is my submission that the early church of the book of Acts experienced extraordinary growth because of these two characteristics. The river of the Holy Spirit continued to flow as the "gifts of the Spirit" and "apostolic leadership" became the banks that enabled the river to flow. Without both aspects making their contribution, I do not believe the church will reach its full potential. Without the gifts of the Spirit the church is powerless, and without the right kind of leadership, the river can easily burst its banks and be lost. It was Jesus who used a similar analogy when he spoke about the danger of "new wine" not being put in the right wineskins and being wasted. *(Matt.9:17)*. It is the main function of apostolic leadership to create effective "wine skins" to contain the wine. These parallel pictures are intended to help the Church flourish by harnessing the power of the Holy Spirit. *(Eph.4:11-16)*

That is not to say that these are the only characteristics that caused the church to prosper. There were, and are, many other aspects of church life that are essential, such as: prayer; outreach; generosity; passion and commitment. All these and more are contributing factors to building strong and healthy churches. However in this volume, I would like to look at the gifts of the Spirit and in a further book called "Pentecost Released" the subject of apostolic leadership.

On one of our School of Ministries trips to Orissa, in India, the local church had advertised a series of meetings on the gifts of the Holy Spirit. They announced them by producing a large banner. Unfortunately, they omitted the letter "f" from the title which meant that it read, "Gits of the Spirit"! Although this was a genuine mistake, this resonates with many of us because we have seen how some churches and individuals have operated and misused these wonderful gifts. I hope the material in this book helps us to understand

2

more clearly the biblical and practical use of these wonderful abilities that heaven has provided for us.

I trust you find the book inspiring, challenging and even a little controversial!.

1

INTRODUCING THE SUBJECT

In my previous book we introduced the gifts of the Holy
Spirit. We spoke of them being released as a result of the
baptism in the Spirit. It was clearly after the Holy Spirit had
come upon Jesus that he began to see the miraculous and
supernatural power of God working through Him. *(Luke
3:21-23)* The statement that *"he began His ministry"* is very
clear. Before that event there had been no miracles, healings
or supernatural ministry. Jesus made that clear as He spoke
of His Divine Manifesto now that the Holy Spirit had
anointed Him. *(Luke 4:18,19)*. Jesus expected to see the
"gifts of the Spirit" evidenced in His life and ministry now
that the power of the Holy Spirit had come upon Him.

It is also significant, that on the same day that the power of the Holy Spirit fell upon those first apostles, supernatural languages poured from them as they were enabled by the Spirit. *(Acts 2:4-21)*. It was this miraculous display of at least fourteen languages, spoken by uneducated and unlearned men, that arrested the attention of the crowd and prepared them to receive the preaching of Peter. It resulted in 3000 coming into a relationship with God.

It is by these gifts of the Holy Spirit that the church continues to manifest the ministry of Jesus. In almost every chapter of the book of Acts, there is at least one miraculous manifestation of the Holy Spirit. It is crammed full of supernatural events and expressions of the power of God.

It is also important to clarify that we are confining our attention to the nine gifts of the Holy Spirit outlined in the book of Corinthians. *(1Cor.12:1:11)*. We are confining our thoughts to the manifestations covered in these chapters *(1Cor.12-14)* but illustrated in both Testaments of the Bible.

I have heard various suggestions over the years, about there being 29 gifts of the Spirit and including various lists from Romans and other places of the New Testament. I realise that the word "charismata" – grace gifts, is used in other parts of the New Testament; and is even used to describe salvation. I am not arguing for only these nine, but Paul the apostle, who wrote the book of Corinthians, seems quite clear that these are the manifestations of the Spirit, and we have enough to occupy our study without trying to find more material.

I would suggest that there are also the Ministry Gifts of Christ, *(Eph.4:7-16)* Which are clearly given by Christ to individuals who are given special abilities to lead the church. This is to be the subject of the next book entitled "Pentecost Released in Apostolic Leadership."

The Father is also involved in releasing different gifts and skills which are related to natural abilities given at birth which can be also used for the Kingdom of God. These are found listed in various places in the New Testament. *(Roms.12:6-8, 1Cor.12:28).* Administration would be among those gifts. We often use the word "talents" to describe these skills.

John Noble, one of the fathers of the Charistmatic movement in the UK, puts it like this, "I have often shared on the fact that every member of the trinity is involved in giving gifts - God is a giving God. The Father uniquely creates natural gifts in each individual; Jesus, the Son, gives us the ministry gifts to lead us in a right direction; and the Holy Spirit gives us the supernatural gifts in order to empower for us to fulfil the commission."[1]

We will look at the subject generally, laying some foundations, before looking at each of the nine gifts individually. I am indebted to some of the fathers of the Pentecostal movement for their teaching and instruction in these matters, but also make my own observations, some of

---

[1] - 'Everyman's Guide to the Holy Spirit the End of the World and You'- John and Christine Noble. (Chapter 6)

which you may agree have a measure of revelation about them, after over 50 years' involvement in charismatic activity.

2

THE PURPOSE OF THE GIFTS OF THE HOLY SPIRIT

I believe these gifts are not an optional extra for the church, but are essential for us both to do the work that God has called us for and to fulfill the purpose of God for the church on the earth.

We understand that the gifts of the Holy Spirit are released to us and exercised by us as a result of us receiving the Holy Spirit. It is by these gifts that the church continues to manifest the ministry of Jesus. When Jesus spoke of "another comforter" *(John 14:6)*. He used the Greek word which means "an exact replica". In other words, the same power, love, character, influence and presence is to be revealed by us as if Jesus were here in the flesh. Our gatherings should be filled with the power and presence of the living Jesus. When He said He would not leave us as orphans but would send the Holy Spirit *(John14:18)*, His intention was that we were to understand that it would be as if Jesus were still among us. We are His body. It is not without significance that Paul speaks of the gifts of the Holy Spirit in the same chapter that he speaks of the church as "the Body of Christ". *(1Cor.12.)* I suggest that if the 9 gifts were in operation in our churches it would be as if Jesus himself were present. It brings new understanding and significance to the phrase "there I am in the midst" *(Matt. 18:20)*. We would truly then be the "Body of Christ". This underlines the importance of pursuing and longing to see these manifestations in our lives and churches. It is sometimes suggested that those with an unhealthy desire for the supernatural or the spectacular pursue these matters, but as I read these passages I see that they are not just important for church life and individual effectiveness, but absolutely essential for us to complete the task to which we have been called. It seems to me that the early church had no problem crying out to God for supernatural manifestations to take place. *(Acts 4:29,30)*. They prayed for "*power*" and for the Lord to "*stretch forth His hand for healing, that miracles, and wonders may be done by the name of Your holy child Jesus.*"

I have the privilege of travelling to many nations in the developing world where the church is growing faster than the birth rate. It is noticeable that the manifestation of the power of God is a significant factor in their effective outreach and the impact they have experienced in their communities. In Uganda, India, the Philippines and other nations, I have met first hand people whose healing ministry has resulted in people who have been raised from the dead, and other outstanding miracles, which has in turn resulted in churches, regions and whole communities turning to God. You will read some of their stories later in the book.

They are grace gifts

The Greek word for gifts is the source of the word Charismatic which has come to describe churches that believe in and practise these Pentecostal manifestations. The word used to describe these gifts, the Greek "charismata", a composite word, which means it is made up of 2 words. "charis" which means "grace" and "mata" which means gifts. *(1Cor. 12:4).* This has come to be a common description used by many around the world. It is very important to understand what this indicates.

They are "grace" gifts; they are not earned, they are not deserved; they are not necessarily an indication of spirituality. They are God's generous, kind, undeserved favours to His people. We will never reach a place where we deserve anything from God. Any "favours" released to us are entirely because of His Grace! I have seen mature believers who have been confused, sometimes upset and even angry when they have watched young converts and immature believers being used by God. God responds to faith. Such activity should provoke us to a jealous seeking for the gifts of the Spirit. *(1Cor. 14:1).* The exercise of these gifts is for all of us whoever we are and whatever status or position we attain. It is only God's generous, undeserved kindness. This is definitely the case with regards to the gifts of the Spirit.

Gifts given for the church

That leads us to understand that although the gifts are exercised by individuals, they are given to and for the church, *"for the common good"; "to build up the church"*. *(1Cor. 12:7,14:4,)* One of the greatest dangers and most common abuses of these wonderful gifts is based upon misunderstanding. I have often heard people state, "I have the gift of healing" or "I have the gift of prophecy". It might sound very spiritual but it encourages pride and self-promotion. I suggest it is biblically incorrect to speak of the gifts of the Spirit being possessed or owned by us. They are the gifts that belong to the Holy Spirit. They are not ours to possess but rather available for us to exercise. We are the human channel through whom the Holy Spirit reveals Himself. These gifts are not given for self-seeking or any other personal ego issue. As the scriptures clearly reveal, they are not for any one individual to be elevated but for all the church to be encouraged and strengthened.

After years of studying this subject, it became clear to me that the language and meaning of the words in the first part of 1Corinthians 12 require special attention. In the first verse of the chapter it speaks about *"spiritual gifts" (1Cor.12:1 NASB)*. In several translations you will see that the word gifts in in italics. This indicates that the word was not present in the original manuscripts but was added as it was considered it would be helpful and make better sense. The Greek word used here is "pneumatikon", which translated literally means "spirituals" or "spiritual matters". The word "gifts" is not implicit or even suggested by this word. A more helpful translation would be something like "Now concerning things which are spiritual" or "spiritual matters". It is suggested that Paul is speaking of more than the gifts in the chapters that follow.

Then again, more significantly, it clearly speaks of the human channel being given the *manifestation* of the Spirit, NOT given the gifts of the Spirit. *(1 Cor.12:7)*. We are all told to expect the manifestation of the Spirit in and through our lives. The Greek word is "phanerosis" which means *display* or *shining* forth. This same word would be used to describe the sun breaking through the clouds. We have all experienced the warm sun breaking through the clouds on a dull, grey day. We can all visualise the warmth and sense of well-being that this brings. The gifts of the Spirit are the "shining forth" of God. They display some aspect of His glory. God communicates and demonstrates something of His awesome person and presence as a "little bit" of God is released. The human vessel is the channel through whom the manifestation of God is revealed.

This leads me to understand that they are His gifts but exercised by people. Those who are used by God in this way are simply the human channel He uses to display some aspect of His person, His character or His power. It is to be noted that it speaks of the Spirit distributing to each one individually as He wills. *(1 Cor.12:11)* Again this suggests that they are His gifts, which he chooses to release through us. He sovereignly releases to one here and one there, one of these supernatural expressions. It is also important to stress that the language is inclusive - "To each one" *(1Cor.12:7,11)*. This is important for every believer to understand. The words are clear that everyone, every disciple of Jesus should be pursuing these gifts and being used by God in such a manifestation.

We manifest His gifts.

My understanding of the scriptures would be that these gifts always belong to the Holy Spirit. They are His, not ours, and he chooses to allow us as human conduits to express something of His glory.

We saw earlier that the gifts are for the common good, for building others up. The gift is not for the person who exercises the manifestation but for the person who receives the blessing. The gift of healing is not for the one whom God uses but it is for the person who is sick. The gift comes from the Holy Spirit through the person who exercises it. The healing is for the person for whom it is intended. The idea of a conduit helps to explain this. In electricity, the conduit is the channel through which the power flows from the source to its destination. You switch the light on and the power travels through the wire and lights the bulb. This is an important distinction. The Spirit sends the gift, using someone to manifest it for the sake of the person who is impacted. They are never our gifts....they belong to the Holy Spirit.

There is a call upon us as the church that God will "bless us to make us a blessing" *(Gen. 12:2, Acts 20:35)*. This is our prophetic calling. The Gifts of the Holy Spirit are one of the ways we bless the world. This calling demands that we are filled with the Spirit, and open and ready to be used by God in manifesting His Glory in the world.

3

DEFINING THE GIFTS OF THE SPIRIT

After teaching on this subject several times, I put together a module for our School of Ministries teaching and training programme. I came up with the following definition for the gifts of the Spirit:

Definition:

"The gifts of the Spirit are a means by which God communicates His power, His knowledge, His presence, His purpose or His Word through the Church to His people and the world, using a human channel."

This long and slightly clumsy sentence embraces the breadth of all that God intends for us through these manifestations. In the following chapters we will look more closely at the subject.

There are nine manifestations of the Spirit.

They are listed in the epistle to the Corinthians. *(1 Cor. 12:8-10)*. In the teaching module I mentioned, I came up with a brief definition for each of the 9 gifts. We would present them as an exercise encouraging the student to come up with the correct definition alongside the gift. Their answers should have been:

1. Discernment — An insight into the powers which motivate certain manifestations.

2. Healing — A divine enablement to heal the sick apart from the aid of natural means or human skill.

3. Tongues — A spontaneous and supernatural utterance in a language not previously learned

4. Knowledge — A revelation of facts previously unknown.

5. Interpretation of tongues. — A supernatural power to understand and then to utter the sense and significance of a message in tongues.

6. Wisdom — A revelation of God's purpose in some special and specific area.

7. Prophecy — Speaking on behalf of God a word of counsel, caution or encouragement.

| 8. Miracles | A supernatural intervention, overriding the regular operations of nature. |
| 9. Faith | A special ability given by God to believe for something extraordinary. |

We will look more closely at these definitions as we examine them individually throughout the book.

They demonstrate the attributes of God.

It is a remarkable and significant but hardly surprising fact, that the gifts of the Holy Spirit express the nature and character of God! After all they are His gifts. Three of the exclusive attributes of God are: that He is Omnipotent, Omnipresent and Omniscient. Which means He is all powerful, always present and has all knowledge. No other being possesses these extraordinary qualities. When the gifts of the Spirit are exercised, one or more of these attributes is expressed.

Remembering our previous teaching, there is a "shining forth" of God. God reveals something of His person and nature through these manifestations. The table on the next page places the gifts into these attributes, giving special attention to this truth.

OMNIPRESENCE	OMNISCIENCE	OMNIPOTENCE
Presence	Knowledge	Power
Gifts of Inspiration	**Gifts of Revelation**	**Gifts of Demonstration**
Tongues	Knowledge	Miracles
Interpretation	Wisdom	Healing
Prophecy	Discernment	Faith
Thought	**Word**	**Deed**

It is immediately noticeable that the gifts are expressed as:

- Inspiration; relating to the presence of God and coming through and from the thought life, the mind.

- Revelation; relating to knowledge expressed by word, speaking.

- Demonstration; releasing power by deed and action.

Imagine a community of God's people fully immersed in the Holy Spirit expressing the fullness and glory of God through and by the gifts of the Holy Spirit. The language of the scriptures is very clear that *"each one"* should exercise the Gifts of the Spirit *(1Co 12:7-11)*. The words *"each one"* occur several times in the passage as well as the phrases *"to one,"* *"and to another".*

Every believer in Jesus filled with the Holy Spirit, according to Paul, is expected to manifest at least one of these gifts. I believe every follower of Jesus should be challenged to desire to be used by Him in this way. We sing songs about "being like Jesus" and "knowing Him" and being "used by Him" about "expressing His love and nature". Through the gifts of the Holy Spirit, our aspiration can be fulfilled as we express something of the glory of God.

4

EXERCISING THE GIFTS
OF THE HOLY SPIRIT

In the light of the challenge, that every believer is to manifest these charisms, I would like to suggest some clues from the scriptures that will help us in that pursuit.

- **Desire.**

Paul encourages us three times to desire the gifts of the Spirit. *(1Cor. 12:31; 14:1,39).*

The context of his encouragement is interesting. I have heard the argument on several occasions that people have chosen the *"better way of love"* as an excuse for not seeking these gifts. This is a very poor interpretation of these passages of the Bible. Paul is not arguing or suggesting that we choose love or the gifts. He is very clear that the *"better way" (1Cor.12:31)* is for the gifts to be operated in an atmosphere and attitude of love. It is not either/or; it is both/and. It is the gifts of the Spirit expressed in love that elevates the gifts to a new level of effectiveness.

I found the following paraphrase for *(1Cor. 14:1)*. It expands the thought of *"desire earnestly"* that appears in most translations. I believe it catches the spirit of what Paul is saying: *"keep on vehemently desiring with a zealous passion that will not abate until you are in full and continuous enjoyment of the gift of prophecy"*. The simple truth is that if there is not any desire there will not be any manifestation of the Spirit of these gifts.

I remember speaking with a mature lady, from an evangelical background, who had lived most of her Christian life without any particular and personal experience of the Holy Spirit. She recognised that the baptism and gifts of the Spirit were biblical and therefore she ought to embrace them. However, having managed for so long without any personal experience of the things of the Spirit, she saw any personal encounter with the Spirit as an imposition on her "normal" Christian life. She would respond to invitations to be prayed for to receive the Holy Spirit out of a sense of duty. There was a hoping it would not happen. The look on her face was of fear and trepidation rather than faith and expectation. I spoke with her, suggesting that she might as well not respond to appeals until she had a desire to be filled. Unless there was that basic desire that Jesus called "thirst" *(John 7:37)*, nothing was likely to happen.

- **Right motivation**

Following on from what we have already mentioned concerning love <u>and</u> the Gifts, not love <u>or</u> the Gifts, we make the statement that for the Gifts to be effective, they must be exercised from a right motive with a correct attitude. It is clear that it is possible to move with a wrong motivation. *(1Cor. 13:1-3).*

It has been well said that; "The presence of LOVE makes our works acceptable to God. The absence of love reduces them to nothing". The suggestion in this passage is that it is possible for the power of God to be evidenced but with the wrong motives which reduces any show of the supernatural to empty, pointless demonstrations. The classic Kings James language of "noisy gong or clanging cymbal" so dramatically expresses the responses many of us have felt when the motivation of the one exercising the gift is suspect. I worked alongside a senior pastor at one time who said that when the motive and attitude of someone was impure or tainted it was like a boil on the face; it was obvious. I understand what he was saying and find myself observing such a situation from time to time. It is the responsibility of leadership and pastoral ministries to help those whose pride and misplaced ambition leads to poor motivation.

- **Hearing from God**

It is imperative that we learn how to hear from God; how to discern and recognise His voice. Jesus was very clear that we could and should hear His voice. *(John 10:4,27).* My wife visited friends of ours who are missionaries in the northern part of Israel. They have a farm and keep sheep. One early evening, during her stay, she was in the field reading, when Steve, who looked after the sheep came to bring them back from the fields where they had been all day. He suggested that Irene call them home. She called but they took no notice. He encouraged her to shout louder; they still completely ignored her. He then began to sing to them. The moment he started singing their ears pricked up; they turned, and began to follow him back to the sheepfold. They knew the voice of the shepherd. I believe God wants every believer to hear the voice of the Shepherd themselves. The people of God need to be taught how to hear from the Lord.

There is an important place for worship and waiting in His presence. There is a place of preparing your heart and being filled with the Spirit. *(Eph. 5:18,19)* The implication of these verses is that we are filled with the Spirit as we worship and sing praise to God. This prepares us to hear from Him as we fill our mind and thoughts with the goodness of the Lord. It is my experience that often the most powerful expressions of the supernatural invasions of the Spirit come in gatherings where there has been extravagant and passionate praise and worship. This is true for our personal times as well. The practise of speaking in the language of the Spirit is important in placing ourselves into a place to receive revelation from the Lord. We enjoyed a visit from Ian Andrews at a time when we were beginning to explore moving in the gifts of revelation. He, at that time was being used powerfully by God. At a leaders' gathering held the morning after an exciting evening meeting, we were privileged to enjoy his teaching again. Given the opportunity to ask questions, I asked for his advice to help us develop in these gifts. His answer was very simple, yet profound. "That's easy", he said. "Speak in tongues for two hours before you come to a gathering and you will find you are open to hearing from God". I still aspire to prepare myself in that way.

The practise of meditation is also a major channel that prepares us to hear from God. David suggests that he receives revelation from this practise. *(Ps.119:97-99);* He describes how he approaches the Word of God. *(Ps.119:18);* learning to wait on the scriptures. He hears the voice of God. I believe that meditation is the place of revelation. Here, more than anywhere, we hear from God. He speaks! I find that the more I imbibe and receive the Word of God in a devotional way, the more I find myself bringing prophetic words and inspiration to others. *"Letting the Word of Christ dwell in you richly" (Col. 3:16)* brings us to a place of hearing from God.

- **Faith**

Faith is a biblical foundation for every spiritual rhythm and discipline. Hebrews lays the foundation for this and declares that it is impossible to please God without faith. *(Heb.11:6).* We have seen that to receive the Holy Spirit the exercising of faith is required. *(Gal. 3:2,14.)* For the nine gifts of the Spirit it is no different. We must cross the fear threshold and move in faith. Every time I find myself in a place where I believe God wants to speak through me or use me, there is a demand to break through the fear barrier and exercise faith. I remember my early excursions in the Gifts of the Spirit. I remember feeling constrained to give a message in tongues. My mouth went dry, my mind was in turmoil as I sought to discern whether this was God or from my own spirit, eventually breaking out in faith speaking out in languages I had never learned, then waiting for what seemed like an eternity until someone brought the interpretation and I breathed a sigh of relief. Even after 50 years of "charismata" I still go through the process of coming to a place of faith. The truth is that you will never exercise the gifts of the Spirit without the exercise of faith. There is a growing in faith that increases as you develop in the exercise of the gifts. *(Roms. 12:6).*

• Action

Faith must lead to action. Leaders of churches must inspire the people into action. Workshops and training events on these matters have been a means for greater release of the things of the Spirit in many lives. Encouragement to people to bring what they have from the Lord from leaders of meetings, is also an excellent way to produce and enable faith to be released. Make room for people to speak out what God is saying to them. Encourage people to open themselves up to God as a channel. Encouraging them that God puts His thoughts into their mind for purpose and making room for that to happen, will make for a greater release of the work of the Spirit. I was recently at a conference on healing where the main speaker was encouraging people to bring words of knowledge. There were some remarkable healings as ordinary believers moved out in faith and spoke out what the Lord was revealing to them. Let us make room for God to "shine forth" among us and reveal himself in powerful ways.

Here are a few practical ways in which people can be encouraged in the release of the gifts of the Spirit.

1. Break into small groups to prophesy to one another.

2. Use the small Group structure for teaching, training, encouragement and development. It is a safe environment for people to learn and make mistakes!

3. Leaders can encourage and make room for people to participate in the main Celebrations.

4. Hold special prayer gatherings for the release of spiritual gifts.

5. Encourage individuals personally, particularly when they are taking their first steps.

6. Make room for personal testimonies; they are a great means of encouragement.

Having laid this foundation, we will now explore each of the nine gifts of the Spirit.

5

GIFTS OF INSPIRATION - TONGUES

Definition:

Tongues – a spontaneous and supernatural utterance in a language not previously learned

The vocal gifts of inspiration express the emotion of God and are related to the release of His Presence. They are utterances, under Divine inspiration, not premeditated or prearranged; they are supernatural and spontaneous as God speaks through them to edify, exhort and comfort. *(1 Cor. 14:3,5)*

The Gift of the Spirit – Tongues. *(1 Cor. 12:10)*

•   **Definition:** "Various kinds of Tongues" is a spontaneous and supernatural utterance in a language not previously learned.

In the previous book we suggested that there are at least six aspects of speaking in tongues. Most of them are related to the use of tongues in our private and personal use. The "gift of the Spirit" is the public expression of speaking in other languages as the Holy Spirit inspires and encourages the individual to speak out. It is often accompanied by an interpretation.

It is in the context of the public ministry that Paul says, "All do not speak with tongues, do they?". *(1Cor.12:27-30).* The passage is related to our different gifting and anointings. It is not a verse to be used to excuse our expectation of speaking with other languages by the Spirit. Many people, baptised in the Holy Spirit and used powerfully by God in many of these nine gifts, have never given a public "message in tongues" in a gathering, even though they speak prolifically in tongues in their personal, spiritual walk with God. One of my mentors, John Philips, a powerful man of the Spirit, would often speak of the fact that he had never been used by God in this way. I myself, have only once, as a young man felt the impression of the Spirit that I should speak publicly in tongues for it to be interpreted. *(1Cor. 12:11,30)* Other are used regularly in this particular "charism".

The word used here is "glossolalia" which simply means speaking in languages. In some versions of the Bible there is a suggestion of something more. This is incorrect and has led to unfortunate and often excessive, ecstatic and weird manifestations. Paul uses an interesting phrase in his epistle. *He speaks of the "languages of men and of angels" (1Cor. 13:1).* I will look later in this chapter at extraordinary examples of people speaking in tongues. They did not understand the language they were using and others in the gathering heard their own, indigenous language spoken. What does the reference to "angels" mean? I do not know but I suggest there are languages that at times we use that have great impact in the "heavenly realm". It would seem to suggest that not all the languages we speak are of human origin.

It is a spontaneous and supernatural act, and the language used is not understood by the one who manifests the gift. It will usually happen, as a person feels and senses an impression of the Spirit, that they should speak out in other tongues. This has usually been restricted to church gatherings, but, as you will see later, I believe there is another dimension we have yet to explore.

Biblical Evidence and examples.

There are various descriptions in the New Testament of "glossolalia".

Mk 16:17 "new tongues"; Acts. 2:4 "other tongues"; 1Cor. 13:1 "tongues of men and of angels";

1Cor. 14:2,14 "a tongue"; 1Cor. 12:10 "different/various kinds of tongues".

The inference from these verses is that these languages are varied, fresh, different and certainly not repetitive or gibberish.

Old Testament Shadow.

There is no definitive example in the Old Testament writings but prophetic examples are evident. The references are used as signs by God as He seeks to arrest the attention of unbelievers.

Paul quotes from Isaiah, as he explains how God used a people who spoke in a certain language style, to work out His purposes. He then suggests that this Charismatic Gift is to be used in a similar way. *(Isa. 28:11, 1Cor. 14:21,22)*

The use of unknown language for God to speak is also seen in the book of Daniel. A hand is seen writing on a wall in the Babylonian palace in an unknown language. This could be seen as an example of God speaking, to arrest the attention of a pagan King and, through the interpretation, to declare His purpose. Perhaps this is rather "writing in tongues". *(Dan.5:5,11,15,24-28)*. Enabled by the Holy Spirit, Daniel gives the interpretation of the message to the King.

New Testament Reality.

It is in the New Testament that we see the full picture. The situation on the day of Pentecost demands our attention. It is the speaking in languages by ordinary, unlearned fishermen that impacts the crowd. The comment is made that these "are Galileans" *(Acts 2:7)*, suggesting they are uneducated. Not one of these early disciples had received any language tuition. They had not visited the local college to study language. There is no doubt that God arrested the crowd through the manifestation of this gift, which in this case did not need an interpretation. *(Acts 2:7-12)*. This supernatural, phenomena opened the people up to receive the word of God. The language suggests they were stunned by what they witnessed. *("Amazed and astonished" Acts 2:7, "How is it?" Acts 2:8, "amazement and great perplexity" Acts 2:12.)* We are told it is a "sign" *(Mark 16:17)*. It certainly was on that spectacular day. Again, the language was not "gibberish" as the people in the crowd declare: *"we hear them speak in our own language the wonderful works of God" (Acts 2:11)*

This initial outpouring, which proves to be a sign as it draws the attention of the listeners becomes a regular occurrence as a manifestation in the life of the early church. *(Acts 2:4-8, 1Cor. 14:26)*. It is interesting to note that it was and is the subject of more discussion and instruction than any of the other gifts. Paul gives more time to explaining its use and regulation then he does to any of the other eight gifts. He explains very practically how it is to be used.

Regulation

Its public use is to be limited because of excess. When we interpret this passage, we should remember that Paul is correcting excessive use of the gifts of the Spirit. I am amazed how many people quote verse 26 in a positive way. What Paul is really saying is that their meetings are chaotic and out of order because everyone has a tongue or a contribution. Their meetings must have gone on for hours. Imagine a meeting of 20 people where each person made 5 contributions. Paul is adjusting their thinking on the matter. I believe this is not a theological issue but a practical one. He is appealing for things to be done *"decently and in order". (1Cor. 14:26-33)*. I think if Paul was writing to most churches today he would be appealing for more participation, and greater release of the gifts of the Spirit with more public utterances in tongues!

I appreciated my upbringing in the Pentecostal movement. I also remember long discussions about tongues and whether different ones should interpret or whether it should be one person. Whether it was acceptable to interpret oneself the tongue one had given. I remember one occasion at a General Conference when all the leaders had gathered together. Due to the numbers attending there were two evening meetings. The General Secretary of the movement, would give the notices in one meeting and then attend the second one. Before he arrived at the second meeting 3 tongues and 3 interpretations had been given. He arrived and the preacher did his job. Following the appeal there was another tongue and the General Secretary stepped forward and interpreted the fourth tongue! The following morning there was a long discussion in the business sessions about this issue. Many were quite animated in their disapproval of this "unbiblical" event. The General Secretary himself said that he would not have interpreted the tongue if he had realised there had already been 3 messages. My personal view is that I am not sure it matters that much. Some of these issues are more like practical guidelines than hard and fast legalistic rules.

Pastoring tongues.

Often bad practise is due to lack of pastoral courage in dealing with excesses and a wrong understanding of this gift. I think most of the problems in public gatherings are down to weak and inadequate leadership. Leaders of churches have the responsibility to oversee and bring direction and teaching in these matters. Not many seem brave enough to deal gently but firmly with those who step outside of the practical, biblical order.

In my late teenage years, I can recall several situations which were never properly dealt with which caused pain and difficulty to many. I believe that there are people in the church who avoid the matter of tongues because of some of these excesses. In one church I regularly visited, there were two ladies who would gradually warm up before they exploded in tongues, sometimes falling off the chair. It sounded like the engine of a steam train getting ready to start on a journey. It was loud, invasive, out of place and completely derailed the meeting. In another church there was one lady who at every meeting tried to give a message in tongues. Many were interpreted, some were prayed over, others sung over but it was never dealt with in a healthy pastoral way. Leaders are to face these matters, bring order, and not allow chaos!

Godward or Manward?

It is quite clear from the scriptures that tongues are man speaking to God and therefore Godward. *(1Cor.14:2,14)*. It is also clear that it is our spirit that prays, by passing the mind. It is a means of communication beyond the natural understanding of man which is initiated by God and encouraged by Paul for all believers to enjoy. *(1Cor. 12:4, 5,*

18, 39)². We will look further into this as we look at tongues together with interpretation.

Reason – Why tongues?

Tongues are a sign to unbelievers, both in and out of the church. *(1 Cor. 14:21,22; Acts 2:12,13)*. There is no doubt that the use of tongues on the day of Pentecost was an extraordinary sign that arrested the crowd as they heard them speaking *"the mighty deeds of God" (Acts 2:11)*. I have heard testimony after testimony of tongues being a convincing, attesting miracle that brought the release of the Word of God and opened people up to the presence and power of God.

I have recently been deeply impacted by the story of the outpouring of the Spirit that began at Azuza Street, Los Angeles. Approximately 30 accounts of tongues being powerfully used by God to arrest people's attention are recorded.³

Tongues are also a sign of the submission of human nature to the Will of God. *(Jas 3:8)*. To speak in languages you have never learned requires us to submit the most unruly member of our body – our tongue, to the Lord. There is a degree of yielding and submission to the Lord that is required, for us to allow the Holy Spirit to speak through us.

Tongues are also a sign of the Kingdom. They have an

---

² See Pentecost Now…Pentecost Then – Peter Butt
³ With Signs following. -Stanley Frodsham.

eschatological significance. The nations divided by Babel are united by the work of the Spirit as they speak together in the language of the Spirit. It is a fascinating experience to be in a gathering of the nations where Spirit-filled believers worship the Lord using the language of the Spirit. There is a commonality, a harmony, a joining of hearts, and awareness of a spiritual connection. It speaks of a future joining of the nations in the eternal ages which repairs the damage of the division caused by the effects of Babel.

Release.

I believe that in the exercise of this gift we simply wait for the impulse of the Spirit; the energising, the anointing. He sovereignly inspires us to speak out. As we sense that prompting we should make ourselves available and working within the boundaries of "*decently and in order*", *(1 Cor. 14:33,40)*, release the message that the Spirit is encouraging us to bring by speaking out in unknown languages.

6

GIFTS OF INSPIRATION –
TONGUES AND EVANGELISM

I believe we have limited our use of tongues to Christian meetings and contexts. I know many Pentecostal and Charismatic Churches where the use of tongues is confined to believers' meetings. *(1Cor.14:20-25)* The verses from this chapter are quoted to that end. However, I would like to suggest another view of this passage. The fact that the uninitiated or unbelievers call us "mad" is not a reason for failing to fulfil spiritual and scriptural exhortations. On the day of Pentecost there were those who suggested the disciples were drunk through imbibing too much wine. Paul, when he shared his testimony before Festus and Agrippa, was accused of *"being out of his mind; that great learning was making him mad".* *(Acts 27:24).*

Many people think evangelical Christians are *"mad"* to believe in the resurrection, the bible and the power of the death of Jesus. The fact that people might express that opinion of us is not a reason to desist. I do believe that in Corinth, Paul, was speaking of excessive use of the gift, where the congregation was going "over the top" on this matter. While concurring that this is not acceptable, I believe we have missed an opportunity and a means of sharing the gospel because of our stance on this matter.

Testimony.

We are grateful to Bill Johnson and the leadership of Bethel, Redding for their encouragement to understand the "power of testimony". *(Rev.12:11)*. We have the biblical example of the use of tongues in evangelism at the birth of the church. *(Acts. 2: 1-13)*. I suggest that it is impossible to ignore the truth that it was the miraculous release of unknown languages that paved the way for Peter to share the story of salvation through Christ alone. This resulted in a magnificent harvest of 3000 people in one gathering, on one day, responding to Jesus!

In recent days I have developed a passion to see this happening in our day. I have experienced the sensation of speaking in languages that others have told me afterwards were known to them. Once in German and again in an African language – Xhosa. The ministry I am involved with means I travel to many different countries. My prayer and aspiration is to be in a context where I speak in tongues in the native language and see people respond to the message from heaven that is conveyed to them by the Spirit. I have even tried to make it happen sometimes but up to now it has not occurred for me. I believe that the Lord wants to use us, in both public and personal evangelism in this area.

Pentecostal outpouring.

I have already mentioned my exploration into the outpouring of the Holy Spirit in the early part of the 20th Century. Azusa Street, Los Angeles is generally recognised as the starting point for this event. I have read many testimonies of tongues being used to convince people of their need of salvation; of people being convinced of the truth of the baptism of the Holy Spirit, of personal messages being conveyed by the Spirit through tongues, and of healing having taken place. In the book, "With Signs Following" by Stanley Frodsham, there are at least 30 accounts of this taking place around the world, in the early days of the last century.[4]

I quote: "A reporter for one of the daily papers was affected during the early days of the meetings in Azusa Street Assembly. He had been assigned to write up an account of the meetings held by those supposedly ignorant, fanatical, demented people. The article was supposed to be from a comical, ridiculous standpoint. He thought he was going to a "circus". After a while a woman gave a call to salvation. She suddenly broke out in a different language. It was the language of this foreign, born journalist. Directing her gaze at him, she spoke of his former sinful, licentious life in the language only he would understand. He was completely

---

[4] With Signs Following – Stanley Frodsham.

dumbfounded. When the service was over, he made his way to the woman. He asked if she realised what she was saying in that language. She answered, "Not a word". This resulted in him committing his life to the Lord Jesus Christ.[5]

The following story occurred in April 1907. Lewis Rudner, a Jew, says," Last winter I was passing a mission building in the city on a rainy day. I saw a sign that said "Welcome", and entered to shelter from the rain. It was a church building and all were kneeling in prayer. The preacher recited the fifty third chapter of Isaiah in the Hebrew language. A woman was singing a song in the Hebrew language, which Jews sing on New Year's Day. A 12-year old girl repeated the 12th Psalm in Hebrew, followed by the 6th Psalm. A woman from Scandinavia spoke in Hebrew, pointing at me, telling me that I was lost, urging me to turn to God. After the preaching, there were again several messages in the Hebrew language, urging me to come and be saved. I asked the preacher if he were a Hebrew. He said, "No, I am German". I told him he had spoken in Hebrew and he was surprised. He had never studied Hebrew. He said that God was speaking to me directly. The woman and young girl then came and spoke again in Hebrew without even knowing the language. I fell to my knees, crying to God for mercy."[6]

There are many other examples with which I could fill the book but one more of a person to person nature is worth a mention. I do believe that God wants to release us into a new

---

[5] With signs following. P32.
[6] With signs following. P208.

exciting dimension of personal evangelism, to expect supernatural encounters. Stories abound about a certain Mabel Smith. (There are many stories of women used by God in the early days of the Pentecostal outpouring, a confirmation of the promise of Acts 2 that on men and women in those days He will pour out His Spirit. *Acts.2:17,18).*[7] Her speaking in tongues was often understood by foreigners. On one occasion, she met a German man who addressed her in the German language. Without knowing a word of the language, she replied in that language and they carried on a conversation in German. The man was astounded and could hardly believe that she did not know the language.[8]

I find this a tremendous challenge in the sophisticated, scientific, rational world of this day and age, would an outpouring of tongues in evangelism be effective? I believe it would!

Let us make ourselves available to God, not just for that impression of the Spirit in a meeting to give a message in tongues, but also in our outreach and sharing of the gospel. I am looking for and believing for inspiring stories of God speaking through various kinds of languages to reveal Himself to lost mankind.

This will take faith and courage!

---

[7] Pentecost Now…Pentecost Then. – Peter Butt
[8] With Signs following. P36.

7

GIFTS OF INSPIRATION –
INTERPRETATION OF TONGUES

Definition:

"Interpretation of tongues" - is a supernatural power to understand, and then to utter the sense and significance of a message in tongues. *(1 Cor 12:10)*

It is interesting to note that the Greek word "hermeneuo" is used to describe this manifestation. This is a word used several times in the New Testament *(John 1:38,41)*, and is the word for translated, describing the process of explaining and interpreting the sense of a word from one language to another. It is also the basis for the word Hermeneutics, which is used widely in the Theological world to describe the art of biblical study and interpretation of the bible: to take the scriptures and explain, expound and interpret them.

The definition, then, is self-explanatory.

Biblical Examples

Old Testament Shadow

This again, with tongues, has no definitive example in the Old Testament. They are the only two manifestations we cannot find examples of under the Old Covenant. This gift along with tongues ushers in the dispensation of the Holy Spirit as an example of a new depth and quality of relationship with God by the Spirit. I suggest it is the outworking of the promise that the Spirit would remain upon us in this new dispensation of the Spirit. *(John 1:33, 14:16,17)*. The promise of a new relationship with God in the future is very clear in the prophetic scriptures. This promise of a new thing must include something different. I believe this is part of that new relationship. *(Jer.31:31-34; Eze 36:26-27; Is.43:19)*.

We have mentioned before Daniel's encounter with Belshazzar. This is closest example we have to this gift, as well as tongues, in the ancient scriptures. *(Da 5)*.

There is the interesting story of Elisha who called for a musician to play and then began to prophesy. *(2Kings.3:15,16)*. The music could be likened to tongues in the sense of bringing the presence of God and providing the foundation for the release of the prophetic word. I mention this because of an experience I had several years ago. We held a meeting with churches across our region, gathering together. The band was made of musicians from several of those churches. During the worship there was a prophetic word to encourage people who needed a fresh touch of the Holy Spirit to come for prayer. As I was hosting the meeting I oversaw the ministry but did not get involved. A lady from the band, who played the violin, went for prayer and then returned to her place in the music team. After a time, the band led us in a song of worship, after which the violinist continued to play a spontaneous song. The melody was rich and powerful. There was a great anointing upon her and the music. It continued for several minutes and at the end there was one of those very special Holy Spirit silences. We held our breath at the sense of His Presence. No one moved. As the leader of the gathering I was asking the Lord what I should do. I felt He indicated to me that this lady, although very proficient, competent and skillful, had never played like that before, soaring into the heavenlies.

This was a result of the anointing of the Spirit she had received in the ministry time. I struggled a little to share this. Going through the usual challenges, I thought, "What if I am wrong?, Am I sure that is this God?" I did share this word and applied it, saying that this was the difference the Holy Spirit makes. He takes our skills and abilities and lifts us to a higher plane. I turned to the lady and said, "You have never played like that before, have you?" I breathed a sigh of relief when she affirmed that this was the first time she had been used in this way.

The relationship with the subject of interpretation is simply this. As she drew her bow across the strings, it was as if the music was talking. I believe I brought the "interpretation" of the music. I am not suggesting we make a doctrine of this but I think we should be alert to "interpretation" being wider than just the translating of "messages in tongues". I am sure many of the Psalms, which have a prophetic edge, came in a similar way!

New Testament Reality.

Surprisingly, there is no practical example of interpretation in the Gospels or Acts either. We are dependent upon the teaching in the account of Paul's letter to the Corinthians for evidence of the existence of this gift in the life of the church. *(1Cor. 14:26-33)*. It was obviously quite prolific in its use, as Paul feels it is necessary to put in some restrictions.

Practical Exercise.

The regulation as to its use is as for tongues and prophecy. *(1Cor. 14:26-33)*. It is stated that there is to be one interpreter for each message. There are various opinions whether one person is to interpret up to 3 messages or whether each tongue should be interpreted by a different person. I am not sure it matters which is correct, although it is most common for one person to interpret all 3 messages.

Operation

The more pressing discussion surrounds the differing views' as to the content of interpretation. Some suggest tongues and interpretation is the equivalent of prophecy. *(1Cor. 14:5)*. The other views suggests that as tongues is "Godward" (i.e. from man to God) *(1Cor. 14:2),* the interpretation therefore should also be Godward. This was the case on the Day of Pentecost when the languages were declaring the mighty deeds of God. *(Acts.2:11).* Certainly, the text of the New International version lends weight to this thought as it translates part of this passage in this way. *"let him interpret what he says". (1Cor. 14:13)* This suggestion would seem to carry more weight, as tongues is prayer or praise. If tongues are directed to God and if interpretation is a translation, one would assume that it should be directed towards the Lord, either as praise or prayer.

Another argument would be this: that If there is no difference, what is the point in tongues and interpretation, why not just prophesy and save time, as they are the same! I certainly lean towards the Godward interpretation. However, I would add a word of caution. There are times in gatherings when we sense that there should be a manifestation of the Spirit but no one is responding. I have noticed that a tongue given at that strategic moment has unlocked a release of the Spirit and there follows a prophetic flow. There has not been an interpretation in the strictest sense of the word but the tongue was relevant and brought a release to others to manifest one of the gifts of the Spirit. Again, I believe it is worth repeating that we have the guidelines from Paul given to a people who were excessive in their behaviour. My feeling is that if he was writing to us in this day he would be encouraging and promoting greater use, not trying to harness our wild excesses.

Tongues and Prayer.

Another area of interest is the use of tongues in prayer. In recent days, I have been going through some difficult situations. I have not really known how to pray. I began to take our little dog for a walk in the early evening, and call upon the Lord. As I walked the streets, I found myself mentioning the name of the person before the Lord and then spending some significant time praying for them in the language of the Spirit. My mind was filled with the burden of their condition but my spirit was praying in tongues. I found a very real sense of strength and help as I pursued this course. On occasions, I even interpreted the tongues in an inspirational way, praying as I felt inspired for that individual. I felt a very real sense of release and relief and of being heard in heaven.

I was reminded of an experience in the 1980's at a Bible Week in Peterborough. The guest speaker was a guy from the USA, called Ralph Mahoney. He spoke on tongues and prayer. He inspired us to see a greater breadth of the use of these gifts. He suggested that we should pray in tongues over a person and then believe for an inspired, prophetic prayer to follow.

At the end of the session we were invited to break into groups and get involved with this activity. I was next to a man, who I was acquainted with but only at a distance. I was not aware of any of the circumstances of his life, or his situation at that time. I spoke over him in tongues and then began to pray the interpretation. I began to pray for him, that as he visited his son he would know the help of the Lord and see God work in his life. I then prayed for his back problem that he would be healed. At the end of the meeting, he came to me his eyes filled with tears. He told me that had been amazing. He was leaving that afternoon to visit his son, with whom he had experienced difficulties and with whom he was looking for reconciliation. He also had a long drive ahead of him and his back had been causing him problems, but as I prayed the pain left immediately.

It certainly worked for us at that time. I must confess that I have not continually practised this aspect of interpretation, but from time to time have felt inspired to do so. I feel challenged to develop this aspect of tongues and interpretation and intend to move in it more in the days ahead. I realise its importance when we are faced with situations and we do not know how to pray!

Release

Again, it is important that we wait for the impulse of the Spirit to propel and inspire us into action. Let us look to overflow with prayer, praise or proclamation as the "Spirit gives us utterance".

8

GIFTS OF INSPIRATION – PROPHECY

Definition: Prophecy - Speaking out of behalf of God a word of counsel, caution or encouragement.

This is a vast subject which has spawned many excellent books in the last 20 years. I have included a bibliography which outlines a number of these volumes, at the end of the book. They are worth reading and studying if you wish to pursue this subject further. I also intend to include substantial writing on the ministry gift of the Prophet as mentioned in the Ephesian epistle under the title, "Pentecost Released" – a fresh look at apostolic leadership. My submission being, that apostolic leadership is about the five distinct ministries mentioned. *(Eph.4:11-16)*. However, in this chapter I am confining my thoughts to what is sometimes known as "the simple gift of prophecy".

Inevitably, we will have to make a distinction between this and the ministry of "the Prophet". There is also some additional material on this issue of prophecy following the definition and explanation of the nine gifts of the Spirit towards the end of the book.

Definition.

According to Paul. This gift of "Prophecy" is speaking out on behalf of God a word of counsel, caution or encouragement. *(1Cor. 12:10, 14:3)*

The Greek word used here is "prophetes" which comes from "phemi" which means *to declare* or *say*. The addition of "pro" simply means before. In other words, it means "to speak on behalf of". The one who speaks is a communicator or conveyor of the heart, mind, will and counsel of God. This is often called the simple gift of prophecy as opposed to the more specific, directional, prophetic word of the person who is a prophet.

The gift of prophecy is not premeditated; it is spontaneous, spasmodic and limited in its content. It is available to be manifested by every believer. It is interesting to note the way the various translations have indicated its purpose. According to *1Cor. 14:3* it is for:

> *"edification, exhortation and comfort" (AV)*

> *"strengthening, encouragement and comfort" (NIV)(NLT)*

> *"edification, exhortation and consolation" (NASB)*

It is not directional, predictive or judgmental. Paul gives clear encouragement to everyone to prophesy. *(1Cor. 14:1,31,39)*. It seems to be a case of "If you desire, you can". It is the ONLY gift that we can all expect to exercise, the only one that we are encouraged by name to desire. I suggest this is because this ability to build up and encourage others is accessible to every believer.

I also suggest that this is because prophecy is a vocal gift that encourages us to develop into other gifts. It acts as a springboard, propelling us to aspire to the "greater gifts" of revelation and demonstration, all of which are exercised by using our voice. Many of us have seen our simple gift of prophecy develop into other gifts: the use of words of knowledge and wisdom, of healing and the release of the miraculous, as our faith has increased through bringing simple words of prophecy. Sometimes we are over anxious to define words as "knowledge" or "wisdom", but the truth is that on many occasions what commences as a word of simple encouragement often develops into something more significant. I love the simplicity of the words of the prophet Haggai:

"Then Haggai, the messenger of the Lord, spoke by the commission of the Lord, to the people saying, "I am with you", declares the Lord". Haggai 1:13.

What a simple, brief word, but full of significance and importance to the hearers! I sometimes wonder if we try too hard to bring a complicated word, full of deep intrigue, feeling the need to impress, when what is needed is a word of *"edification, exhortation and comfort"*. I remember hearing Graham Perrins describe much Pentecostal prophecy as "a passing thought through an empty head". I understand what he was saying but I have been astounded to see how a simple word of encouragement has impacted people's lives.

On one occasion, I was preaching in a church in Wickford, Essex. Their usual musician had not been able to attend and I ended up on the keyboard. A young lady walked in during the service and sat down. I felt the Lord drop a simple word in my heart for her: "God loves you, knows all about you. He cares about you and your circumstances". Following the worship, as I was invited to speak, I shared this simple word with the young lady and she began to sob uncontrollably. One of the ladies ministered to her, and following the service she shared her story. She was not a follower of Jesus. That morning she and her husband had a very serious argument which resulted in her leaving the house and declaring that she could no longer live with him. There were many issues which had resulted in this breakdown of relationship.

As she walked the streets, wondering what to do, she passed the church and heard the singing. She felt this urge to go in the building; that the answer to her dilemma was in this place. She had never visited the church before but in response, walked into the building and sat down. I then shared that simple word, which opened her up to the Lord. She made a commitment that morning to surrender to the Love of God and became a part of the church. I could have felt the word was too simple and tried to embellish with my own thoughts and opinions. It was simple, relevant and exactly what was needed at that time.

Biblical Examples

Old Testament Shadow.

Most of the prophetic ministry of the Old Testament was predictive. The example already quoted from Haggai is a parallel with the New Testament gift of the Spirit. There are also parallels between the Old Testament and New Testament prophets but there are also distinctive differences, which are covered in the additional material at the end of the book.

New Testament Reality.

What is surprising is that there are no definitive examples in the new, except in the teaching of Corinthians where it is emphasised that this gift was in regular use in the church. *(1Cor, 14:3,26)*. It is interesting that we read of Philip's daughters *"which did prophesy" (Acts 21:8)*, and several verses later we read of *"a prophet named Agabus" (Acts 21:10)*. It is important to state that because God has used you in a word of encouragement, that does not make you a prophet. Over the years I have seen people used in the simple gift begin to imagine they are "prophets". Difficulty and confusion have followed.

Practical Exercise.

There is again a regulation on the use of this manifestation.

There is this suggestion of a maximum of 3 separate words of prophecy in a public gathering. I believe this is for the sake of order, to correct the excessive use in Corinth. Most meetings I attend I feel moved by the Lord in some area of the prophetic. I think I could bring a prophetic contribution in every gathering I attend. Often, I find that if I wait, there is an opportunity to share the word with an individual and sometimes with the gathered company. We should learn to meditate on the word and listen for the prompting of the Spirit regarding its purpose and timing.

What is clear is that there are those whose responsibility it is to discern the prophetic flow, and oversee the correct and orderly flow of prophetic ministry in the church. There is to be an affirmation of the prophetic from those in the church who have a mandate for this task. *(1Cor. 14:29)*. The word judgement can seem rather harsh. The intention is rather to discern and make decisions, not to bring a sense of condemnation.

However, it is important that we give a clear encouragement to prophesy. *(1Cor. 14:31)*. We also want to avoid any extreme responses to the prophetic in our churches. We are not to resist, despise and thus quench the Spirit, which is a wrong response. Neither should we accept unreservedly, without judging and weighing any prophetic contributions. This is also a wrong response. *(1Th 5:19-21, 1Cor. 14:29)*

Distinction.

It is important to mention the distinction between the

prophet and prophecy. The prophet is an office by divine appointment. A prophet would be part of a leadership team. It is a permanent ministry at the prerogative of Christ. This person is particularly and purposefully called by Christ into this ministry. Its outworking includes: words of knowledge and wisdom, visions, dreams, preaching and teaching. Revelation often comes through waiting upon God. *(1Cor. 12:28, Eph. 4:11).* As we have clearly stated, the simple gift of prophecy is not premeditated. It is spontaneous and limited to encouragement, strengthening and comfort.

Challenge.

If we can *"all prophesy one by one" (1Cor 14:31).* The question must be; "Have you prophesied yet?"

If not, why not?

9

GIFTS OF REVELATION –
THE WORD OF KNOWLEDGE

We now turn to the gifts of revelation. These express the Omniscience of God - His knowledge. God is all knowing. There is nothing He does not know. We are limited in our knowledge and understanding and come to the end of human wisdom, knowledge and understanding. By these gifts of revelation, we can find answers that bring release and healing. We understand situations and apply the knowledge that God gives us to fulfil our calling as His body on the earth. We will look first, then at "a word of knowledge"

Definition:

A Word of Knowledge is a fragment of God's knowledge given to a person by the Holy Spirit. It

gives information and certain facts not previously known by the person or attained by natural means. They are given by supernatural revelation of the Holy Spirit. *(1 Cor 12:8)*

At a recent healing conference I attended, the emphasis on the word of knowledge was related to healing. The teaching and training encouraged those attending to hear God regarding some of the different ailments and sicknesses represented in that meeting. Towards the end of the gathering, people in the congregation were invited to come to the microphone and call out various physical problems. Many did so. Some were very general words like "someone here has a back pain"; others were very specific, with details of dates and times, operations and medical history. There was a response to many of these words and several people testified to healing.

I must confess, I do struggle with the more general words, as in a congregation of 500 there are inevitably a number with back problems. I also accept that people do have to start somewhere, and as they develop and their faith increases, so does their revelation. However, I digress. The main reason for mentioning this example is that many will identify with what I am saying and have been in similar situations. I believe in this practise and would want to encourage it as one aspect of the word of knowledge.

My concern is that, if that is all the word of knowledge is, it is a very limited expression of this gift. In fact, there are very few biblical examples of "a word of knowledge" in the area of healing but a proliferation of other examples of this gift of revelation. I trust our horizons and expectations will be enlarged and expanded to see this gift in greater fullness, as we look further into this gift.

"A word of knowledge"

It is important to emphasise the description of this gift. It is not the ability to have on-going insight and constant revelation. It is not just an increased knowledge achieved through study and experience. It is the ability to receive a fragment of God's knowledge; it is a supernatural download of information from heaven.

There is no definite article in the Greek. It is therefore "a" minute portion of the vast treasures of knowledge that belong to the Godhead. *(Is. 58:8,9; Col 2:3).* In our introductory chapters we mentioned that the gifts of the Spirit express each of the unique attributes that belong exclusively to God. We said that God is Omniscient. That means He is all knowing. There is nothing He can learn because He knows everything! In this gift He reveals "a" word, a little of the knowledge that He has. We need that knowledge to fulfill our purpose on the earth, or for God to bring about some intention of His own will. Many people quote the promise made in the book of Jeremiah:

Jer.29:1. "I KNOW the plans I have for you, says the Lord, plans for welfare and not for calamity, to give you a future and a hope"

The problem for us is that we do not always know what

those plans are. It is often through a word of knowledge that He reveals something of those plans to us.

Biblical Examples

In the Old Testament, the Holy Spirit comes upon individuals. Many of the prophets, priests and kings exercised this gift of the Spirit. In the New Testament, we are all kings and priests and are encouraged to use the gifts of the Spirit. There are many examples in both Testaments of God revealing His knowledge to his people.

Word of knowledge in the Old Testament.

Samuel, the prophet, receives knowledge from God that he could not have possibly known outside of supernatural revelation. He receives insight regarding Saul's anointing as king and the whereabouts of his donkeys. *(1 Sam. 9:15-20)*. There is an astounding clarity and quality of knowledge concerning the things Saul is about to experience. *(1 Sam. 10:1-8)*. Later in the same chapter, Saul's whereabouts is discovered using this gift. Samuel receives knowledge of where Saul is hiding to avoid being pronounced King. *(1 Sam 10:21-23)* The specific nature of these words of knowledge is quite outstanding and distinctly miraculous.

David's sin is exposed by the Word of Knowledge as Nathan the prophet uncovers David's action in seeking to hide his sinful behaviour with another man's wife. *(2 Sam 12:7-9)*.

Elisha receives revelation about the actions of his servant

Gehazi. He directly disobeys the instruction to take no reward from Naaman. Elisha receives supernatural revelation of his activity. His sin is uncovered by this extraordinary word of knowledge. There is nothing vague about these words; they are always clear and distinct and undoubtedly from God. *(2Kings 5:25-27).*

It is interesting to note how often a word of knowledge is expressed in the ministry of a prophet in the Old Testament.

Ministry of Jesus

It is when we look at the ministry of Jesus that we see the greatest examples of the use of this gift. The gospels are full of examples of extraordinary, supernatural revelation pouring from the Lord Jesus as He moved in the power of the Holy Spirit. What is interesting and revealing is the number of times this gift is exercised when Jesus is dealing with unbelievers. It is the nature of the revelation that initially arrests their attention and opens them up to the gospel. We so often think of miracles and healing as the means by which God arrests people's attention, but in several of the cases mentioned below it is the word of knowledge that draws a response from the hearer and leads to their salvation.

- Jesus affirms and confirms the healing of the centurion's servant as He receives revelation from the Father. *(Mattt.8:13)*

- Jesus confirms that the daughter of the Syrophoenician woman has been released from demonic activity, even though the child is not present. This could only happen because of a word of knowledge. *(Mark 7:29,30)*

- A word of direction concerning the whereabouts and provision of a colt for Jesus to ride into Jerusalem. The disciples are given instructions which come from Jesus by revelation. *(Mark 11:2,3)*.

- There is a certain irony here as a carpenter tells a fisherman where to find fish. Only God could have known where the shoal of fish was located. *(Luke 5:1-7)*

- Nathaniel is overwhelmed by the revelation of facts as Jesus tells him where he was, and even which tree he was sitting under, before he met Jesus. *(John 1:47-50)*. This clearly opens Nathaniel up to the truth of who Jesus is and leads to his becoming a follower of Jesus.

- The woman at the well is astounded by several words of knowledge that Jesus shares with her. She is convinced by the revelation of this information, that Jesus is a prophet, and comes into a relationship with Jesus as a result. *(John 4:18-20)*.

These are just a few examples of the proliferation of this gift in the life and ministry of Jesus. There was nothing spooky about it. He lived in such a close relationship with the Father that he constantly heard His voice and responded accordingly. *(John 5:18,19)*.

Ministry of Early Church

Then again, we see in the life of the early church, many clear and distinct manifestations of words of knowledge in the church.

- Peter receives supernatural knowledge from heaven in exposing the hidden sin of Ananias and Sapphira. This is not guesswork or human intuition or deduction. It is a clear word of revelation, not just of the facts but also of the source of their deception. *(Acts 5:1-6)*.

- Ananias receives extraordinary information about the whereabouts and situation of Saul. He receives clear and distinct Divine guidance as a direct download from heaven. *(Acts 9:10-20)*

- In the story of Cornelius the Roman centurion, and Peter the church leader, there are clear words of knowledge, giving information, direction and instruction. *(Acts 10:1-33)*

- Agabus, who is described as a prophet, receives a word of knowledge concerning a coming famine. *(Acts 11:27,28)*

This gift is seen in the early church on numerous occasions. Listening for the voice of God and responding to His instruction provided a bedrock of faith and support for the believers in those days.

The church today.

I am convinced that God would release more of His knowledge to us today if we were listening more intently.

During my years of ministry there have been many times when I have been in a place to hear from God. He revealed by the Holy Spirit information that I could not have possible known.

When I was a pastor in North London in the early 1970's, a young couple came to faith in Christ. The husband was a baker and had to be at his work by 4am every morning. They were just starting out and not able to afford a vehicle, so it was important for him to live near his workplace. The young woman was speaking with me one Sunday about their need of somewhere to live. She described how they were becoming very concerned and frustrated at the lack of suitable accommodation. I responded as I felt the Holy Spirit inspire me. I said that if they would honour God, the Bible was clear, He would honour them. I invited them to attend the prayer gathering on the Tuesday evening and said that if they honoured God He would provide a place for them to live before the end of the week. This was either a word from God or a foolish act of presumption on my part. They came to the prayer meeting; we prayed for their situation.

The following day the woman was returning from her place of work and decided to buy a bar of chocolate. As she left the underground train station, she did not turn right as was her usual practise, but turned left and walked a few yards to a shop selling confectionery. At the moment she arrived, the shopkeeper was placing a card in the window advertising an apartment which, of course was perfect for this young couple. They viewed it that evening and occupied the flat before that weekend.

While I was leading that same church, we embarked on a building program. We were a small church and the members engaged in as much of the building work as we could manage. We required 6 new interior doors and found that they were going to be very expensive. I was concerned about this and whilst driving in the area was praying and asking God for His help on the matter. I felt Him say to me to stop my vehicle and visit the builder's merchants I was passing at that moment. He said they had the doors we needed. I admit I struggled with this information and wondered how to speak to the storekeeper when I entered.

I explained my predicament to the owner of the business who immediately broke into a smile. He took me to the back of the storeroom and showed me 6 doors, all brand new, painted, and with the hinges all attached to them. He explained that a carpenter had bought these doors and hung them in place only to discover he had put the hinges on the wrong side and this had made the doors unfit for their purpose. They were perfect for us!. He gave me all 6 for £6 as they were no use to him. A little word of knowledge can go a long way! And save a lot of money!

Recently I visited Sheffield. While in this city, the leader of a church requested that my wife and I spent time with him over a coffee. I was intrigued by his interest in meeting up. We spent some time together and he said that 14 years ago I had spoken in their church. During the message I had shared what I believe was a word of knowledge. Apparently, I had said they were not to worry about their building, which was becoming too small, because God was preparing a palace for them. A few weeks later another prophetic ministry had passed through and said that God was giving them a building that would be half the price and three times the size. For 14 years they carried these words and prayed over them. Just 2 years before our meeting, a building had become available. It had been a Bingo hall. They made an offer for the building and acquired it at a much lower price than expected.

When they entered the building, they discovered it seated 3 times the number of people their present building accommodated. They then sold their building for far more than they anticipated and worked out that the new building had cost half the price of the sale of their old meeting place, exactly as the word of Knowledge had indicated. When they began work on the building, they sought to restore the front façade to its original state. They discovered it had been a dance hall before it was a Bingo Hall. They, then discovered it had originally been a cinema called "the Palace". Imagine their surprise at the fulfillment of the word of knowledge. This was such confirmation of the leading of the Lord that increased their faith and confidence that God was with them.

Purpose.

At the beginning of the chapter I mentioned that we are in danger of relegating this manifestation to healing when it is intended to have a far wider impact. I suggest it has the following applications:

- To bring people to God. It draws people into a relationship with God. We have seen how, with many in the life and ministry of Jesus the word of knowledge breaks them open to respond to the good news. It is a major evangelistic tool that we have yet to embrace in our evangelism.

- To uncover sin. Sensitivity is required if God reveals a word of this nature. Clearly in the case of Ananias and Sapphira there was a public exposure of their sin but reading carefully the text we do not know the full context of the story. *(Acts 5:1-11)* Normally, when sin is being uncovered, these words should be given sensitively to avoid embarrassment. It is also important to give people an opportunity to respond and put things right. I remember receiving a word of knowledge, while ministering in Belgium. It was concerning adultery. I shared the word in a public gathering that God had seen what had been done in secret but was giving the perpetrators an opportunity to respond and repent before he allowed their sin to be shouted from the rooftops. I suggested that they seek counsel from their leadership in private. That evening a couple came for ministry as the husband had confessed his misdemeanour to his wife that afternoon and we had the joy of praying with them for reconciliation. They later became leaders of the church. During that next week the leader advised me that at least 3 other couples had come for prayer and sorted out their broken marriages. I returned to the UK, and was surprised when one of the men from that church in Belgium, called me. Later in the week he arrived at my home and asked for help with his past moral failure as he was looking to clean up his life and follow the Lord.

- To give guidance and direction. Some of the examples given above are of God specifically and distinctly bringing the knowledge of His will and purpose for a certain situation.

- To minister encouragement in periods of difficulty and despondency. The empathy of a God who knows and understands, revealing His knowledge of our present situation, is a tremendous help in difficult times. Paul was in a life-threatening storm on a ship when he received a word of knowledge followed by a word of wisdom. This caused the preservation of his own life, along with 276 others. *(Acts 27).*

- To impart knowledge of future events. The scripture used above is an excellent example of this.

- To reveal hidden things. Again, we see this in the story of Ananias and Sapphira.

- To quicken faith for healing. We have already endorsed this aspect of the word of knowledge.

Practical exercise.

There are characteristics of this supernatural gift that are worthy of attention. As with all the gifts of the Spirit this manifestation comes by faith and demands the exercising of faith every time you move in it. Again, as we exercise faith we grow and develop in this gift. I believe that, from the basic gift of prophecy, we see the emergence of words of knowledge and other gifts as our faith increases in our hearing from the Lord.

This gift is usually received in your spirit. It can be a vision, dream or picture. With regards to the healing aspect it sometimes manifests as a pain or sensation in a part of the body.

Except in very rare occasions the gift requires a vocal expression. The word must be communicated to bear fruit. We need to speak out what God has revealed. This is where a step of faith is required.

I have discovered with increasing regularity, that during preaching I will receive a word of knowledge; something I have just said to the whole company has specific relevance to an individual. During this recent season as I have been expounding on *Acts 2:17*, where the promise of God is for

"Our sons and daughters to prophesy" I have encouraged individuals by name to expect God to touch their children and bring them back into relationship with him. I have not known the people or their circumstances but have been encouraged as these parents have confirmed the "word" concerning their children that I shared with them. I believe there are many occasions when the preacher, under the anointing of the Spirit, says things that have dramatic and personal significance to a hearer and are an expression of this gift. We may never know how many times that has occurred. When I am preaching I often emphasise a truth I have just shared as I feel the Spirit nudging me that this is a word for a person in a particular situation.

I think more than anywhere else, we need sensitivity to the voice of the Spirit when we are involved in counseling. We need to look and listen whenever we are praying for someone. My wife has been involved with healing prayer clinics over the years and seen how important the word of knowledge is in many situations.

On one occasion the Lord helped her as she visited a woman who was dying as a result of breast cancer. She had decided not to have surgery, and although she had been prayed for over a long period of time she had not been healed. She had become angry with God and felt let down and was struggling in her faith. In her confusion she had requested a visit from my wife. As my wife walked to the ward, she asked the Lord for help. She had no confidence that the woman would be healed but rather that she was going to die. As she sought the Lord she felt Him say. "There is no death for the believer; it is life or life. There is either physical life now or eternal life in heaven. There is no death for you. Whatever life God has chosen for you, you will be healed!"

As she shared this the lady responded positively and she was restored in her relationship with the Lord. She died a few days later in a place of peace and faith. A group from her church worshipped around her bed just a couple of days after my wife's visit and she felt able to join with them expressing her love for the Lord. No amount of words or even theological truth would have met her at that time but that word of knowledge caused her to break through.

We want to see and recognise more of this gift in our personal lives and churches. It produces: conviction, confirmation, repentance, restoration and increases faith. I believe it is one of the greater gifts Paul encourages us to desire. *(1Cor.14:1)* Let us go for it. believe for it, exercise it and see God work among us, and particularly for those who are not yet walking with Jesus.

10

THE WORD OF WISDOM

Definition:

The Word of Wisdom is a fragment of Divine wisdom supernaturally imparted by the Holy Spirit. It supplies one with the immediate wisdom to know what to say or do in each situation. *(1 Cor. 12:8)*

Wisdom comes out of knowledge. As we understand the information; wisdom knows the correct course of action to take. It is the application of knowledge. It is expressed as knowledge applied in the best way to bring a solution to a situation. It is interesting that it is the first in the list of the gifts. Isaiah, speaking of the coming of the Messiah, speaks of the anointing of the Holy Spirit that will be upon Him and in the sevenfold expression of that empowering lists *"the spirit of wisdom"* as the first quality. *(Is.11:1-5)*. Does that suggest it is first in importance? I would not want to come to that conclusion except to say we do require a dose of "the wisdom of God" in every aspect of our lives and ministries. Certainly, wisdom is required to minister in all the gifts in the right way at the right time, with the right motivation of love.

As we look at examples of this gift, we note that it is closely aligned to knowledge and there is often an overlap of the two gifts. Sometimes a word of knowledge leads to a word of wisdom. The information received leads to revelation as to the right course of action to take. I have been in situations where one person has the word of knowledge and another has the word of wisdom to apply the truth that has been revealed. Another important distinction to make is that it is not human wisdom or wisdom that comes from experience and understanding. We are clearly told to pray for this. We often describe this as common sense. *(James 1:5)*. The word of wisdom is when God clearly reveals the way ahead and speaks clearly of what we need to do.

Biblical Examples

In the Old Testament there are numerous examples of this gift. Often God revealed His wisdom in dreams. (I believe that dreams often come under this category.)

- Pharaoh, the king of Egypt had several dreams that he felt were significant. He did not have any understanding of what they meant. *(Gen.41:1-13)* Joseph, who at that time was in prison, was summoned and asked to interpret the dreams. He interpreted Pharaoh's dream using supernatural wisdom given by God. It is interesting to note that he first brings a word of knowledge of what the dreams mean – a word of knowledge. *Gen. 41:14-32).* He stated that there are to be seven years of plenty, followed by seven years of famine. He then brought a word of wisdom, as he instructed Pharaoh on the solution to the problem, and the course of action that was to be taken. *(Gen. 41:33-37).* The response of the King was fascinating, since he recognised that Joseph has been enabled by the Holy Spirit to interpret the dreams. *(Gen.41:38,39)* He then appointed Joseph to oversee the project. *(Gen.41:40-49).*

- Solomon is faced with an impossible situation. Using his natural powers of deduction and human wisdom there is no solution to the problem. Two women stood before him, both declaring that the one baby belonged to them. One baby has died but both mothers are claiming this baby as their own. Solomon's word of wisdom, supernaturally given, solved this impasse and causes the people to recognise that "*the wisdom of God was in him*". *(1Kings 3:16-28)*

Ministry of Jesus

The greatest demonstration of this gift is in the Lord Jesus. He was filled with the Spirit of wisdom as we have mentioned above. *(Is.11:1-5).* We see on many occasions Jesus drawing on this wisdom to refute false teaching, answer questions and deflect the wrongly motivated accusations of the leaders of the Jewish people. Many times, when His accusers attempted to trap him, his reply completely flummoxed his antagonists. *(Matt. 21:23-27)*. When faced with the temptations in the wilderness at the beginning of His ministry he receives Divine wisdom as he quotes appropriate truth from the Word of God which refutes the accusations and insidious suggestions of Satan. *(Luke 4:1-13)*. He gives answers to questions which express the wisdom of God. When the scribes and chief priests ask Jesus a question which to the natural mind is impossible to answer, the scriptures say, *"He DETECTED their trickery"* There was revelation, not just the ability to come up with a clever answer. Luke writes, *"they were amazed at His answer"* *(Luke 20:22-26)*.

Ministry of Early Church.

In the book of Acts, we see this gift expressed in the life of the church, as they seek to grapple with issues that arise among them, that are beyond their natural abilities. In the early chapters of this book, it is interesting to note the many times Peter or one of the other apostles take Old Testament scriptures and receive revelation, applying that passage into the dispensation of grace and the fulfillment of the purposes of God through the church. *(Acts 2:16-21; 2:25-28; 2:34,35; 3:25; 4:25,26; 7:6,7; 7:27-50; 13:41; 13:47.)*

When we read through Paul's epistles, we are again aware of the many references to the Old Testament Scriptures as he receives the "wisdom of God", applying the truth of the

Old into the context of grace and truth that comes with the advent of Jesus. There are so many examples that even a brief excursion into the books Paul wrote will reveal the extent of this gift, as he writes inspired by the Spirit. Consider his classic declaration in Ephesians that *"the mystery which for ages has been hidden in God that the manifold WISDOM of God might NOW be made known through the church....in in accordance with the eternal purpose which He carried out in Christ Jesus our Lord" (Eph. 3:8-10).* This underscores the fact that this manifestation of supernatural wisdom is being released from heaven.

Knowledge and wisdom in partnership.

It is in the Acts that we see, perhaps more clearly than anywhere else, the working together of the word of Knowledge and the word of Wisdom. The story of Ananias and Sapphira provides that example. *(Acts 5:1-12).* This couple have agreed together to mislead and lie to the church leaders concerning their giving of money. Peter receives a word of knowledge about this and reveals this information. *(Acts 5:3,4.)* Notice, it is just the facts. The result is that judgement falls on Ananias and *"he fell down and breathed his last".* Later, his wife Sapphira enters the room. Peter asks a question based on the knowledge he has received regarding their behaviour. When she confirms their agreed lie, his response is to bring a "word of wisdom"; He does not just reveal the facts but reveals what is going to happen to her. Because of this situation, he declares that she will also forfeit her life. *(Acts 5:8-10).* I guess it does not really matter whether a word is knowledge or wisdom but as the two gifts are mentioned by Paul separately it is intended that we are able to discern the difference. I think I am appealing for us to move in these areas in the "Spirit" rather than be spending too much time discussing them!

Practical Exercise

There is an obvious need for the release of this gift among us. It is essential for solving problems. We need keys from heaven that will unlock difficulties. I know I have been in leaders gatherings, where we reached an impasse. We did not know what to do. We found ourselves at a loss as to the way ahead. Then one of the team received a "phanersosis" from heaven. Light came into our confusion, and there was that moment of hearing the wisdom of God for the matter. There is a cry of, "That's it!", and we moved ahead with confidence that God has broken into our lack of understanding with His wisdom.

As we have seen, we can depend on this gift for dealing with opposition and debate. It is also important for strategy for the future. As I am writing, I am reminded of King Jehoshaphat of Judah, faced by a massive enemy and its army. *(2Chron.20:1-30)*. Along with the people, he cries out to God. Their words echo down the ages. *"We do not know what to do, but our eyes are upon you" (2Chron. 20:12)*. The wisdom of God comes from heaven in response to this prayer through the prophet. *(2 Chron.20:14-17)* Not only does he assure them of the help of the Lord, but also gives them the strategy and plan for defeating this enemy. The wisdom given defies the natural order. It results in an extraordinary demonstration of God's power as they carry out the instructions from heaven.

Characteristics.

It is like the Word of Knowledge, in that it is received in the Spirit and often comes as a picture, vision or dream. Again, it can often come as a part of a simple word of Prophecy. I believe God also releases His wisdom in preaching and teaching and many have testified to hearing "a word" that has unlocked their confusion and provided an answer to their dilemma.

We spoke of healing and the word of knowledge. There is also a place for Wisdom and healing. I mentioned my wife and her ministry before. She tells of a young man who came to the Prayer Clinic with a smoking problem. His health had suffered badly and the doctor had warned him that if he did not quit this habit it would eventually finish him off. He came to the clinic in despair having tried everything he knew to get free. As my wife prayed for him she felt God give her a word of wisdom to provide the man with a solution. It was simple but profound. She shared with him what the Lord revealed to her. She said, "Water is a type, a symbol of the Holy Spirit. You need the help of the Holy Spirit to be released from this habit. Every time you have a desire to smoke a cigarette, have a glass of water instead, and ask the Holy Spirit to help you to overcome this addiction". He returned the next week to say he had not had one cigarette and that his health was already improving.

This continued for a several weeks until he knew he was free from the habit.

What is the point of healing if our lifestyle will cause the sickness to return? Perhaps we need as much wisdom when we pray for people as power. I remember a lady, many years ago, who was seriously overweight and quite unwell, requesting prayer. My father, who was leading the gathering, felt the Lord say, "Tell her to stop taking sugar". He shared this word; she responded by saying that she had 5 teaspoons of sugar in her tea and loved her sugar. No amount of prayer was going to resolve this situation! Let us learn to listen for the wisdom of God.

The exercise and use of the word of wisdom is imperative in these days, when so often we feel like Jehoshaphat and do not know what to do. Leaders often need a supernatural revelation of wisdom beyond the use of general wisdom, for specific issues in the church.

I have mentioned before my friend, Simeon Kayiwa from Kampala, Uganda. He tells the most amazing stories of extraordinary miracles. Often there is an aspect of wisdom related to the outworking of the supernatural intervention of God. He tells of a woman from Entebbe, on the bank of Lake Victoria, who had recently been converted. Her husband was a violent drunkard. He had expressed his displeasure at his wife's salvation and was threatening her with violence. She came to Simeon and expressed her fear and asked for advice. As Simeon listened to the Lord he felt the Lord say that, Within 3 days God will intervene. She had no need to fear; she should return home and the Lord will work and change the situation." He shared this with the woman who responded positively and went home to find her husband drunk in the house and threatening violence. When he discovered she had been to the church, he flew into a rage, took the purse, removed the money, went out to the banks of Lake Victoria, threw her money to the left and the purse to the right and said, "Let us see if your God can provide for you". Three days later the fish seller came through the village carrying Tilapia and Nile Perch in a net on his back. She went out and chose some fish for their dinner. When she came back into the house her husband was sitting on a chair in the corner in an angry, drunken state. She placed a fish on the table, cut it in half, and there in the fish was her purse. Not only that, but when she opened the purse, her money was inside. The husband was watching and when he saw this, he was completely overcome. He sorted out his life, became a follower of Jesus and planted a church on the banks of Lake Victoria of which he became the leader!

We do so much counseling, giving advice as best we can. Perhaps it is time to look for more of this supernatural wisdom being released to us. Some of the issues we are facing in these days, particularly with regard to sexual morality, which require more than just "chapter and verse". I pray that God will grant us His supernatural wisdom.

We can do no more than agree with Paul as he prays for the church at Ephesus. We pray that *"the Father of glory may give you a spirit of wisdom and understanding and of revelation in the knowledge of Him. I pray that the eyes of your heart may be enlightened so that you will know...." (Eph. 1:17,18).*

11

THE DISCERNING
OR DISTINGUISHING OF SPIRITS

Definition: Discerning of spirits is the supernatural capacity to discern from spiritual insight whether the spirit operating has a source that is human, demonic or divine. *(1 Co 12:10)*

I find it fascinating that the gift is not described as the deliverance, or casting out of demons; what is commonly known as exorcism. This gift is the ability to distinguish the source of activity, whether it is human, demonic or divine.

It seems that authority to set people free is given to the believer. According to the passage in Mark's gospel it is faith that is required for exorcism. *(Mark 16:17)*. This is significant as Jesus suggests that some demonic activity is so entrenched that it takes serious prayer, even with fasting, to release people from the bondage of satanic oppression. *(Matt.17:19-21)*. The casting out of evil spirits and deliverance from demonic forces is not to be treated lightly. In the story of the early church in the book of Acts. There were some who saw Paul in action and thought they would try their hand at deliverance. They were not in a position to engage in this ministry and found themselves overpowered by the man with the demon. *(Acts 19:14-17)*. However, all believers walking in relationship with Jesus, are encouraged to confront demonic activity wherever it raises its ugly head. So we can then make the assertion that this gift of the Spirit is "discerning" or discovering the source of the activity in order that appropriate action can be taken.

Over the years there have been many books written on this subject. Conferences have been convened, training courses been undertaken. I have noted different emphases and fads over the years. Some of them, I believe, have been counter-productive and have brought fear and not release. Some of the methods of discerning the root of spiritual activity have been more like diagnosis then discernment. It is suggested that certain physical responses are an indication of demonic involvement. I find this difficult to embrace as there is no biblical record or evidence of these things.

I remember some 30 years ago experiencing some pins and needles in my hands during worship sessions. I spoke with a leader who suggested this might be an indication of several areas of demonic activity in my life that required attention. I allowed him to pray with me, being a novice in this area.

Nothing happened. It was a while later, when these symptoms continued to occur, that I had a conversation with a doctor. He asked me if I raised my hands in worship. This was during a special season when we were experiencing extended times of worship. I replied that I was lifting my hands in praise in a way I never had before and for considerable lengths of time. He then explained that the pins and needles were simply the blood draining from my hands because of holding them above my head for long periods in worship. That's does not mean that physical signs are never an indication of demonic activity, but I do have problems with this kind of prescriptive discernment.

It is interesting that in the original Greek, the word "spirits" is plural, but also the word translated "discernment" or "distinguishing" is plural. I believe this is emphasising the need to distinguish between the human, demonic or divine. The source of any activity can be any one of these or perhaps even a mixture. In these days, with the advances in medical science, we see that there are occasions when manifestations can seem demonic when in fact they have a perfectly simple medical explanation. People suffering with diabetes can undergo personality changes when the sugar level in their body falls below a certain level.[9]

---

[9] HYPOGLYCAEMIA (LOW BLOOD GLUCOSE) . NHS WEBSITE ON DIABETES.

If you have diabetes, your blood glucose levels can become very low. This is known as hypoglycaemia (or a "hypo"), and it's triggered when injected insulin in your body moves too much glucose out of your bloodstream. Symptoms of a "hypo" include: feeling shaky and irritable, sweating, tingling lips, feeling weak, feeling confused, hunger, nausea (feeling sick). A hypo can be brought under control simply by eating or drinking something sugary.

I have seen sane, ordinary people react in ways that could be construed as demonic when suffering from low blood glucose. Extraordinary damage has been done by making outrageous claims that this behaviour or that response is an indication of demonic possession. We recently held a conference on an issue of moral, sexual behaviour and again deliverance has been attempted on people because of, an assumption that their behaviour was rooted in demonic possession.

As a leader in the church I have had to deal with numbers of people who had some form of epilepsy which has led certain people to practise deliverance on them. As no deliverance came and nothing changed they had been left in confusion and often fear. This condition often has a medical foundation and is treated by the appropriate medication. We should rather be praying for healing to take place. I believe therefore, any deliverance should only take place based on discernment. Receiving revelation from God is the basis for setting people free. There may be, of course, some expressions of epilepsy that may well be demonic in origin, which is why the correct use of this gift is so important.

Biblical Examples.

I am surprised that there are no definitive examples of this activity in the Old Testament. Not one clear example of discernment or of exorcism is to be found. Although there are references to demonic and satanic involvement and occult practises, there are no clear illustrations of either discernment or deliverance. The nearest example is perhaps when   Eli discerns the voice of God. *(1Sa 3:1-9)*. Whether he received this revelation by revelation or intuition is uncertain but the same word "discern" is used to describe his recognition that God is speaking.*1Sam.3:8)*. Samuel himself receives revelation when seeking the Lord's choice for the next king of Israel and he discerns the nature of men by revelation. Perhaps this is an example of the gift of distinguishing spirits. *(1Sa 16:6-13)*.

Ministry of Jesus

It is when we look at the ministry of Jesus the manifestation of this gift is exemplified through His life and ministry. On many occasions people who were demonised would manifest in His presence without any need for this gift of discernment. On other occasions Jesus expresses this gift in his dealings with people. On one hand Peter is praised for discerning the divine and then rebuked for expressing the demonic. *(Matt.16:17-23)* Recognising the source of that which comes from "the flesh" (is human in origin) or "Satan" (the demonic) is important for us in making decisions as to what motivates people.

Another area that is open to misuse but very clear is that the source of sickness can be demonic. In *Luke 13:11-17* Jesus was very clear that this sickness was caused by a spirit. In several translations it is called *"a spirit of infirmity"*. He further declared that this woman had been bound by Satan for 18 years. There are other examples of sickness being caused by the attachment of a demonic spirit to a part of the body. Jesus rebukes a deaf and dumb spirit in the case of the young boy who cannot speak or hear. *(Mark 9:17-29)*. On other occasions in the gospels the mention of both the healing of the sick and casting out of demons are mentioned in the same verse. There is a clear distinction. *(Matt.4:40,41; 8:16; Mark 1:34)*. This accentuates the need for revelation. Some attribute all sickness to demons.

I do not believe that this is a healthy, biblical stance as there are only a few examples in the gospels of sickness being attributed to spirits. There are numerous references to healing the sick. I find it interesting that when Jesus sent out the 12 he gave them four different instructions for various ailments, which suggests they all came from a different source. *"He said, Heal the sick, raise the dead, cleanse the lepers, cast out demons" (Matt.10:8)*. Perhaps we should take a little time before we minister and pray for the needs of people to allow the Spirit to speak with us and give us discernment.

Ministry of Early Church

In the early church, we do not see as many cases of demonic activity as there are in the life and ministry of Jesus. That is not surprising. However, we do have several expressions of this gift recorded in the life and ministry of Paul. In Paphos Paul and Barnabas encounter opposition. Paul by the Spirit discerns the root of the opposition. Revelation comes as he fixes his gaze on this man Elymas and is filled with the Holy Spirit. The marginal reference of the NASB translation is interesting. It suggests and alternative but correct translation would be *"having just been filled with the Holy Spirit."* The sense is that at that very moment, the inspiration of the Holy Spirit is on Paul as he exposes the source of his opposition and calls blindness upon him. *(Acts 13:9,10)*. In the other example we find Paul exercised by the activity of a slave-girl with a *"spirit of divination" (Acts 16:16-18)*. Luke, the writer clearly describes the spirit that motivates this young woman. He would only know this because of revelation. Paul moves against the source of this fortune telling and brings deliverance to the young woman. It may also be that this gift is helpful in the exposing of false prophets. The church in Ephesus are commended for that. *(Rev. 2:2)*.

Practical Examples

We increasingly need this ability to discern between good and evil, spirit and flesh. We certainly do not want to waste time chasing demons that do not exist. For many years my wife and I were involved in running youth camps. One night we were called to a room where a young lady of around 15 years of age was showing all the symptoms of demonic activity. Apparently, she had tried to throw herself out of a first-floor window. She was thrashing about and making all kinds of noises as she screamed and shouted at the top of her voice. Several other young women had gathered around her and there were several youth leaders present, some of whom were trying to hold her down and shouting at what they thought was a spirit. It was chaotic!

As the leader of the ministry I felt a sense of responsibility but was not comfortable with the scene before me. Not being convinced that this young girl had a problem with an evil spirit, I asked the Lord for some wisdom and revelation. She was wearing a baseball cap. As I was listening for the voice of the Lord I watched as her baseball cap fell from her head to the floor. She stopped all her thrashing about, bent down, picked her hat back up and started "manifesting" again. I thanked the Lord for that insight, stopped all the prayer and sent the crowd that had assembled out of the room. Along with the youth leaders responsible for the girl, I spoke with her according to the revelation the Lord had given me about her need for attention. She received the word and responded with tears as she quietly allowed us to minister to her.

This business of hearing and discerning the voice of God is very practical and we need the help of the Spirit in the judging of prophecy. Sometimes its source is the flesh; the human spirit. I believe we will increasingly experience revelation concerning angelic activity. We need to discern the presence of angels and the purpose of their invasion into our realm. The discerning of the nature, names, numbers and activity of demons is a practise which should be approached with care and caution. It is very subjective and based upon very flimsy biblical evidence.

The exercise of this gift can come in several ways: simply a word, the inner knowing of the spirit, or we may be feeling uncomfortable. This is often a signal from the Holy Spirit and we need to wait for revelation. This of course, can be true of places as well as people. Seeing shadows or light can often be an indication of demonic activity. Sometimes the enemy has a grip on the soul of a believer which needs attention. This gift will help discover any areas of oppression in people's lives. It is particularly important in the areas of counseling and prayer for the sick.

What about Principalities and Powers?

An area that I would suggest needs investigation and consideration, which I have not heard anybody else speak of, concerns the matter of what has become known as territorial spirits. I would suggest that there is a link with this gift of the distinguishing of spirits. There has been much recent teaching and discussion in the church about the Spiritual forces that dominate the heavenly, spiritual realm. *(Eph.1:21, 6:12, Col.1:13-16)*.

Conferences, books, ideas and opinions have been produced over the subjects of "Identificational Repentance"; over the issue of whether it is biblical to address principalities and powers directly; often also "Spiritual mapping" is encouraged to discover the spiritual forces that operate in a town or region. Is it possible that the answer to these issues is that this is what this gift of the Spirit is also for?

We have often limited this gift only to concern the activity of the demonic in individuals. Perhaps we have reduced its breadth and use? It seems to me that it would simplify all the confusion and fanciful ideas concerning these wider matters if we waited for "discernment" and only addressed these issues on the basis of revelation. We would not then have to come up with obscure and somewhat dubious biblical interpretations for our activity.

I suggest that we should only engage in these matters when God reveals by the Spirit that atmospheres and activities in towns, area and regions are caused by demonic hierarchies. When I read of the success of this ministry in places like Argentina, I note that the significant men and women of God that engage in this kind of prayer warfare spend days waiting on the Lord for revelation. It is on that basis that they proceed with prayer that clears the way for the presence and power of God to be revealed.

Just a thought for us to consider!

12

THE GIFTS OF DEMONSTRATION – GIFTS OF HEALINGS

Definition: A divine enablement to heal the sick apart from the aid of natural means or human skill. *(1 Cor. 12:9)*

One short chapter cannot possibly deal with this vast subject. I can only introduce the subject and point you in the right direction for further study. I guess it is important right from the beginning to mention that we are only dealing with healing as it relates to the Gifts of the Holy Spirit. There are other foundations for healing and differences in practise. There are various biblical administrations of healing. What I mean by that are that there is a variety of ways and reasons that healing comes. The following aspects of healing are healing by or with the "Gift of the Spirit". These healings happen on a different basis.

There is healing in the Church. When a member of the church is suffering, they are encouraged to call for the leaders of the church, who are instructed to anoint with oil and pray the prayer of faith. *(James 5:14-16)*. We are told healing takes place because of the prayer of faith and the confession of any faults by the person being healed.

There is also an encouragement for those who believe to lay hands on those who are sick. *(Mark 16:17,18)*. It is clear from the text that this healing is in response to faith. The context of the chapter has to do with preaching the gospel and evangelism. There is the expectation that "signs and wonders" will follow the proclamation of the word of God. *(Mark 16:20)*. The word "signs" means "attesting miracles". The suggestion is that God proves and attests to the truth of the message by manifesting his power in healing and miracles. It is a sign to those who do not believe of the reality of the person of Christ.

Then again there is healing through the use of medicine. The source of all healing is God. He has put the resources in the earth for the healing of the nations. Interesting to note in Ezekiel the reference to leaves being the source of healing *(Eze.47:12)*. Many natural resources have healing properties in them. The leader of our church network is Billy Kennedy. He has an interesting view of what seems to be our unanswered prayer regarding people with cancers. We have seriously and persistently prayed for people over the years to be healed of this dreadful disease and a few have been healed but many died. However, over the past 20 years the advances in medical science mean that the statistics of those healed has risen amazingly. Many of the various forms of cancer are now being healed. With some forms of this disease twenty years ago 80% died and 20% survived. Those statistics have been reversed, and many now survive. Billy's view is that every prayer we have released to heaven has been heard and answered by God in revealing to the medical researchers the keys that have caused the healing of cancers to increase.

The subject of what is called "Healing in the atonement" is very current. This was a strong emphasis in the early Pentecostal movements. The Assemblies of God held it as one of their fundamental truths for many years. Again, it is a vast subject, but my understanding of this matter is that healing is available because of the atonement but is not "in the atonement" in the same way as salvation. Everything we receive from God is because of the work of redemption through Jesus on the Cross of Calvary. He truly did carry all our sins, sickness and pain when He died for us. My reading of scripture suggests that we are still waiting for the fullness of that salvation for our physical bodies; they are not yet redeemed (*1 Cor 4:6, Roms 8:23*), but God in His grace and because of His lovingkindness, releases healing to us.

I believe the gifts of healings are another form of healing but there are differences from those listed above. In the above ministrations of healing all are encouraged to share and to believe. However, when it comes to gifts of healings,

Paul is quite clear that not all participate although all are encouraged to desire. *"all do not have the gifts of healings, do they?" (1Cor. 12:30,31)*

If our general teaching on the gifts of the Spirit is correct: that the gifts belong to the Holy Spirit and we are the channels who exercise and manifest them; then the Gifts of healings are immediate and must be complete. If a Gift is given, it must work: The Gift is perfect; our faith is not. If it is the gift of the Holy Spirit and it is resident, then everybody must be healed, but that clearly is not so. So, we make the statement that when a gift of healing is given, it is for the person who is sick not the person who is used by God in dispensing it.

Donald Gee, that great Pentecostal statesman, said, "There is a mistaken idea that if possessed of the gift of healing, one could enter any hospital and heal every sick soul". Jesus left some sick at Bethesda, passed by the man at the Beautiful Gate, and Paul could not cure Timothy and left Trophemus sick at Miletus". The only example I have come across of someone emptying a hospital ward is in the ministry of John G. Lake. It is recorded that on one occasion he felt inspired to pray for every sick person in that room and they all left their beds and were all healed.

Peter's shadow brought healing only when there was a special anointing for healing upon him and Paul performed special miracles only in Ephesus. The inference is that you can only release this Gift effectively when the anointing is upon you. However, we are encouraged to lay hands on the sick and exercise faith in the on-going work of the church for both believers and non-believers.

It does seem that there is a special release of healing in certain contexts. Many of the examples in the life and ministry of Jesus, when it declares he healed all that were sick, are related to public gatherings which we would describe as outreach meetings. *(Matt. 4:23-25, Luke 4:40,41)*. There is clearly a special anointing when in an evangelistic context which I suggest is the outworking of signs and wonders following the announcing of the good news; a confirming of the truth in special releases of healing. I have just been reading of Stephen Jeffreys, the Pentecostal evangelist used by God powerfully in the 1920's and 30's. Astounding miracles were released as he travelled around this nation.[10]

Regarding the gift of the Spirit, it is very interesting that it is the only Gift where both words are plural, "gifts of healings". What does this indicate? Some suggest a gift is given on a special occasion for a specific sickness. I think a better understanding is that each separate healing is a gift from God. When God moves us in this way, it must work. As we have said, we cannot heal at will. We do not possess this gift but can only move in healing when prompted or moved upon by God. We know when it happens.

I have been in meetings where the preacher has suggested that the Lord is present to heal those with back problems or

---

[10] Seven Pentecostal Pioneers. P.47

some other ailment at that meeting. I have been in gatherings where the host has suggested that there is no healing anointing present for that gathering and has not prayed for those present who were sick. I do not agree with this as I believe we are encouraged to pray, lay hands on the sick, anoint with oil and exercise faith. However, as I have indicated I do not believe that form of healing is this gift of the Spirit.

My experience in this gift over 40 years is simply that there have been occasions when I felt that surge of faith and knew I carried a gift of healing. I remember praying for a lady with an arthritic condition. As I went to lay hands on her I distinctly heard the Lord say to me that I should lay my hand on her back. As I did so I knew she had been healed. I did not say a word; there were several of us praying. After praying, I asked the woman how she was. She replied that when one of those praying had put their hand on her back, instantly all pain had left and she knew she was healed. I believe I received a gift if healing for that woman.

I was recently in a gathering in the USA and an older lady suffering with dementia was present. She had not been lucid for several years. Her husband was distressed by her condition as she did not recognise him. As we were praying generally, I felt a surge of faith to pray for her. As I did so, she began to pray clearly and with clarity. She then sang a song and followed this with a prophecy. Her husband was beside himself with joy as tears flowed from his eyes. I have never, before or since, seen that happen. I believe at that moment I was in a place to hear from God and move in this gift. I wonder, if we were more in tune, whether we would see more of the release of healing in this way.

My conclusion, as with so many of these charismatic gifts, is that gifts of healing should be exercised on the basis of revelation. It certainly is not the ability to heal at will. It is interesting that some of those used powerfully in healing have been sick themselves. I read of Stephen Jeffreys, the Pentecostal evangelist, used powerfully by God in the 1920's and 1930's. His son, Edward reported, "In his own bedroom, he was prostrated with weakness, but an hour later was on the platform preaching with amazing power".[11]. This man who saw 1000's of extraordinary miracles suffered from severe arthritis for the last years of his life. It is reported that he would stand to preach bent low by the pain in his joints and that as he preached he would straighten up and see God work powerfully in healing the sick, but following the meeting would return to his former state.

Recently, I was in conversation with my friend Basil D'Souza from Mumbai, India. He was sharing how in his experience, he finds healing often associated with and prompted by another gift of the Spirit. A word of knowledge or wisdom, supernatural faith or discernment, or even prophecy can be the springboard for healing. The link between healing and other gifts of the Spirit is very strong.

[11] Seven Pentecostal Pioneers – Colin Whittaker p.71

Biblical Examples

In the Old Testament, one of the clearest incidents is the remarkable healing of Naaman. Elijah the prophet brings a word of wisdom that results is this man being instantly healed from the life-threatening disease of leprosy. *(2Kings 5.)* Hezekiah, the godly king, is another example of a clear and distinct release of healing. *(2Kings 20:1-11)*

The ministry of Jesus is shot through with numerous examples. It is noticeable how many of the following scriptures include the words "immediately" or some similar phrase. These are just a few of the healings of Jesus in the early chapters in Mark's gospel. *(Mark 1:31,41, 2:12, 5:29, 42, 7:35, 10:52).* Any of the other gospels would reveal this gift operating in the ministry of Jesus. They are indications of Jesus living out his declared intention to *"only do the things He sees the Father doing" (John 5:19,20).* Perhaps if we were living in a more intimate relationship with the Father, we would hear His voice and be prompted in this gift of healing.

In the ministry of the early Church in the book of Acts, we see this emphasis again. The first recorded miracle of healing takes place in the temple area. Peter and John are going to pray. A man who has been lame from birth calls out to them requesting silver and gold. Their response is to fix their gaze on this man and call him to look at them. Peter then releases a gift of healing to the man. His words are very revealing. He says, *"What I have I give to you" (Acts 3:6-8).* He knew he had something to give the man. He had that sense of authority and confidence to promise the man he would be healed. It was as Peter was "filled with the Spirit" that he was inspired to impart healing to him. They had passed this man many times before as they had gone into the temple but his time they were carrying a gift of the Spirit. On another occasion Peter is "filled with the Spirit" for a task. If you have an NASB reference bible you will notice the marginal reference gives the alternative rendering as "having just been filled with the Spirit" (Acts 4:8). This suggests there was an unusual sense of God coming upon him at that moment for a purpose. I believe that is how the gift of the Spirit is released. There are also the special miracles that occurred through both Peter, *(Acts 5:12-16)* and Paul. *(Acts 19:11-12)* These were extraordinary healings. This was not the common or usual way healing took place.

Practical Exercise

My attempt to look at this vast subject may have left you with more questions than answers. My intention is for us to desire earnestly to see this gift in operation. *(1Cor.14:1)*. My encouragement would be to pray for the sick as we are commanded, and as we are praying generally to look for signs of God moving and listen for the prompting of the Spirit.

Sometimes our hands will feel hot, sometimes a burden will come upon us, occasionally a feeling or a pain, or some other sign. However, when God moves on us there will always need to be a step of faith. Let us continue to learn to hear the voice of God in this matter and see an increase in supernatural healing among us.

13

WORKING OR EFFECTING OF MIRACLES

Definition: "A miracle is an orderly intervention in the regular operations of nature; a supernatural reversal or suspension of a natural law." *(1 Cor. 12:10)*

The word Paul uses for miracles as a gift of the Spirit is *"dunamis"* which is translated throughout the New Testament as *"power"*. A miracle, then, is an act of power. From the beginning of the scriptures God is revealed as "Omnipotent" – all powerful. His acts of power are both destructive, (in the case of judgement), and creative, when He intervenes positively on behalf of His people. In the opening of the Red Sea we see both aspects of the miraculous. Creative: the opening the Red Sea to provide a way of escape from their enemies. Destructive: the closing of the Red Sea on the pursuing Egyptian army in judgement. Paul then expresses the fact that we can expect to see God's power manifested on our behalf through this gift.

We then read of the disciples, commissioned by Jesus. "*And going out, they proclaimed everywhere, the Lord working with them and confirming the Word by miraculous signs following. Amen*". *(Mark 16:20).* When we read the phrase "*signs and wonders*", this is often a reference to miracles. A sign is "an outward visible indication of power". A wonder is "an extraordinary occurrence, appearance or action." The NASB marginal reference makes this clear as it ascribes the words "attesting miracles" to the phrase "signs and wonders". *(Mark 16:20, John 4:48, Acts 4:30).*

It is sometimes quite difficult to differentiate between the three gifts of power. There are many similarities between this gift and healing, and often an overlapping with the gift of faith. There are occasions when it is difficult to distinguish between them. When someone is raised from the dead, we would often call this a miracle. However, they probably also need healing as the cause of death is usually sickness, so healing must take place for them to stay alive. Many also suggest that it takes supernatural faith to raise the dead.

Healing or miracle?

Personally, I do not think it is essential to define the difference between healing and miracles too distinctly. As we have seen from our previous paragraph, there are examples where there is an overlap of the gifts of power. By our common use of the word, we have often spoken of a miracle when healing has taken place, which is not strictly correct. A simple distinction, to help us, is that healing is restricted to the human body and related to sickness, whereas miracles have a much broader application into the physical world. Perhaps as we look at miracles in the scriptures we will see this more clearly.

Biblical Examples

In the Old Testament there are many miracles but two particular periods when miracles were prominent. In the life of Moses there was a proliferation of miracles. His call to leadership was established when his shepherd staff; turned into a serpent as he threw it to the ground. *(Ex. 4:3)* The 10 Plagues were all examples of the miraculous power of God being displayed. Moses held up his rod following instruction from heaven and was used by God in the miracle of the opening of the Red Sea. *(Ex.14:16)*. There are so many miracles during the wilderness wanderings: Water from a rock; a serpent on a pole bringing healing when they looked on it; Miriam's leprous hand becoming whole; the rod that budded; and many more.

The second period of miracles occurred during the life and ministry of Elijah and Elisha. These two prophets of God saw extraordinary signs and wonders during their ministries In the first chapter, describing Elijah's ministry, we have the miracle of proclaiming a drought, the provision of food from ravens, the provision of food from the jug of oil that kept producing and the raising to life of the widow's dead son. *(1Kings 17.)* From this chapter through to the conclusion of Elisha's ministry, every page is jam packed with demonstrations of the miraculous power of God. *(2Kings 9.)*

When we turn to the New Testament, miracles are in abundance in the life and ministry of Jesus. Alongside the healings there are also many miracles. Jesus calmed the sea. He spoke to the storm and it ceased. *(Mt 8:23-27);* On at least two occasions he fed a crowd of at least 4000 and then 5000 with 5 loaves and 2 fish. *(John 6:1-14).* There is the miracle of turning water into wine. *(John 2:1-11).* Producing money in mouth of a fish to provide the finance to pay their taxes. *(Matt 17:24-27).* The raising of Lazarus from the dead. *(John 11:1-46, 12:18).* Jesus walking on the water, defying the natural laws of gravity, is an outstanding example of a miracle. *(John 6:19)*

Miracles are in evidence in the early church. It is interesting to note the activity of angels in the deliverance of Peter from prison. Doors open, chains fall off, gates are opened as Peter is led by an angel from the prison *(Acts 12:6-11).* Elymas is struck with blindness as Paul speaks to him, which is another remarkable miracle. *(Acts 13:6-12)* Paul shakes a poisonous snake from his arm as the snake bites him. The watching crowd are amazed that he does not die but remains alive. *(Acts 28:3-6)*

Purpose of miracles.

Miracles are seen throughout the scriptures as necessary for any of the following reasons:

- Preservation: Daniel's three friends are thrown into a fiery furnace that is heated to an extremely high temperature. The only thing burned is the ropes their hands are tied with. The three men are not burned in the furnace. The king sees a fourth man in the fire whom he describes as like the son of God. *(Dan 3:25)*. Many of us can also testify to seeing God work in our lives to preserve us in miraculous ways.

- Provision: This story in the life and ministry of Elijah illustrates how God provides for us in miraculous ways. A small amount of oil and meal keep flowing for them as long as they need it. *(1Ki 17:12-16)*. One of our connections in India is in the state of Orissa. During a time of severe persecution several years ago, the church members found it necessary to leave their homes and live in the jungle. While in the forest, the only means of communication was by mobile phone. However, there was no electricity to re-charge their phones. They felt the Lord showed them a large leaf. As they rubbed their phones against this leaf their phones were re-charged. This continued for many days. As soon as they could return to their homes and acquire electricity again it stopped working! God is still in the business of providing miraculously for our needs.

- Deliverance: In the story of the opening of the Red Sea that we have already mentioned, we see the miraculous power of God demonstrated. *(Ex 14)*. Many of our African friends tell us amazing stories of deliverance from all kinds of attack, physical and spiritual. One story concerns an assassin sent by a gang to shoot one of the pastors. In the meeting, as he tried to draw the gun out of his pocket, his hand froze. When he released the gun, he could draw his hand out. He tried several times to take the gun out and shoot the pastor. At the end of the service one of the ladies went to the pastor and said she had seen a circle of angels around him during the meeting. He did not take any notice of this until the next week when the man returned and told his story. This miracle resulted in the assassin's salvation.

- Discipline: There are numerous examples of miracles relating to discipline and judgement. We have already looked closely at the example of Ananias and Sapphira *(Acts 5.)* In the Old Testament, Jeroboam the king experiences similar restriction to the account in the last paragraph as his arm is paralysed by a miracle. *(1 Kings 13:1-6)*.

The challenge for us, is to raise our expectation to see the increase of miracles among us. Paul encourages the Galatians with an exhortation to look to *"the God who works miracles among you" (Gal 3:5)*. Obviously, miracles were a common occurrence in the life of the believers in the early church. It seems to me we need to place ourselves in situations where we will see this gift operating among us.

14

FAITH

Definition: A special ability given by God to believe for something extraordinary. *(1 Cor. 12:9)*

It is important to clarify the different aspects of faith. There are other aspects of faith seen in the scriptures. This gift of supernatural faith is *not*:

- Saving faith. This is the faith we exercise to believe God for salvation. *(Acts 16:31, Eph. 2:8)*. The moment when the reality of the truth about Jesus comes alive in us as we believe that Jesus died for our sins to bring us back to God and into relationship with Him.
- Living faith. This is the kind of faith we exercise when praying or living out our spiritual life. Every day we believe God for our safety, protection,

provision and general well-being. We are encouraged to pray over every detail of our lives and pray in faith, expecting and believing God to work on our behalf. The basis of our faith is that *"the just shall live by faith"*. *(Roms 1:17)*. The verb in this verse is in the present continuous tense, which suggests that we not only come into relationship with God through saving faith, but also continue to enjoy and explore our relationship with God by faith. Like the disciples, we pray for an increase in this aspect of faith. *(Luke 17:5)*

- The Fruit of the Spirit. Then there is the fruit of the Spirit, which in many versions is translated; faithfulness. The meaning of this word has more to do with loyalty, persistence, steadfastness; it is an aspect of character. *(Gal 5:22)*

Faith as a Gift of the Spirit.

This is faith given for a special need; it is a supernatural deposit to believe for something extraordinary. Donald Gee, one of the early Pentecostal leaders, described it in this way: "It would seem to come upon certain of God's servants in times of special crisis or opportunity".[12] I was impressed by the picture presented by this definition of the gift by Aaron Linford: "The gift of faith may catapult ordinary faith to a higher plane of trust in God, supernaturally or momentarily."[13]

---

[12] Concerning Spiritual Gifts – Donald Gee. p.36
[13] Spiritual Gifts – Aaron Linford. p.55

I believe Jesus was speaking of this gift when he encouraged us that in the moving of mountains this kind of faith is required. The literal rendering of the verses relating these passages in the Gospels is *"Have the faith of God". (Mark 11:22,23).* It takes faith of the kind that God possesses, to take us to a new level of believing. It is a magnification of ordinary faith to extraordinary proportions.

Biblical Examples

It is often difficult to distinguish between miracles and faith. Often both are required in the same event. When Joshua commands the sun to stand still and then repeats the same instruction to the moon, he assumes a divine prerogative. *(Jos 10:12,13).* I suggest that an act of this nature can only be carried out when we have been inspired by God to exercise this supernatural faith. In the New Testament, Paul assumes amazing faith and makes a startling declaration. *(Acts 27:22-25).* According to the account, they have been in an extraordinary storm for days, the ship is breaking up, even the sailors are afraid, there is no land in sight and Paul declares they will be fine. His statement, *"I believe God",* suggests this is a special faith that has been released to Paul for this situation. Elijah declares that it is about to rain. He makes this statement when the sky is blue, there is not a cloud to be seen and it has not rained for 3 years. *(1Kings 18:41-45).* I suggest we can only make announcements and declarations of this nature when this gift of faith is released to us.

Practical Expression.

It is worth considering when this gift might be required by us and where it might be necessary. It would seem to be deposited by God at specific moments for specific tasks. I would suggest a few places where it is required. I believe it is essential when we are believing God for extraordinary amounts of finance. I know of church leaders who have embarked on building programmes way beyond the capacity of their expected finance. I have heard many stories of extraordinary miracles of supply coming from unexpected sources. I have also, sadly, seen building projects fail, churches lose their way, and even close, where a project was undertaken without that Word of the Lord that increases faith and confidence in God's provision.

This faith is required for a project that defies the natural order of things. It seems to me that believing for weather to change demands this kind of faith. The stories of Bible weeks and rain abound. We prayed, believed, shouted at the devil, did just about everything we could think of to change the weather but the rain persisted. It seems as I read the biblical account that an extraordinary deposit of supernatural faith is required for actions such as this.

There is a faith, beyond the ordinary faith that comes by prayer, that can see a nation change. God can deposit faith in the heart of men and women to believe for breakthrough in towns, cities and regions, even nations.

I have seen this kind of supernatural faith exercised in

Uganda. Our friend, Simeon Kayiwa from Kampala, leads a church in Namirembe, and oversees a network of churches throughout the nation. He tells of a situation that arose during the difficult days of the Amin regime. The people were afraid for their lives and so gathered at the church building to spend the night together. There was no food in the shops; people were hungry. Around 150 gathered each night. Simeon, concerned for their well-being, asked the Lord what he should do. There was a mango tree on the church grounds. It had never born fruit, although it was a large tree. The Lord told him to speak to it and command it to bear fruit. The next day it was covered with mangos, and every day there was a new crop until food appeared in the shops and then it ceased. I have seen the tree myself and others have confirmed this miracle that I believe was a result of the gift if faith.

This same man has seen several people raised from the dead. I have personally met several of them. The stories are intriguing. In every case there is a clear word from heaven that inspires faith and results in people being raised from the dead.

One lady was involved in a road accident. She was severely hurt and the driver did not know what to do. He stopped a taxi and requested that the lady be driven to the hospital, having paid the fare. The taxi driver soon noticed that the lady who was seated upright, had fallen over. He stopped, examined the body and found she was no longer breathing! A crowd had gathered and one of them indicated that the woman was part of the church at Namirembe. The taxi driver saw this as a way out of him having to explain what he was doing with this lady in his cab, and so drove to the church. He entered the pastor's office with the lady over his shoulder. He put her on his desk, said, "I believe this lady is from your church", and disappeared as fast as he could. Simeon walked around the room, praying and asking God what he should do. The answer from heaven was for him to speak to the body and command her to come back to life. This he did; life returned immediately and she sat up!

Her testimony was remarkable. She described how she had left her body and went through an awful darkness before entering a place of beautiful light. There she met Jesus, who explained to her that she had experienced what it was like to be separated from God, but that she had to go back and warn others to turn to Christ and know salvation. As Jesus said this, she heard Simeon's voice calling her back to life. She returned to her body and sat up. She has been giving her testimony around Kampala and many have been challenged to give their lives to the Lord. I believe activity like this requires the gift of special faith.

Our encouragement must be to earnestly desire the greater gifts. Jesus did promise us that we would see greater works *(1 Cor. 12:31, John 14:12)*. I guess that must include a few resurrections!

15

WHERE DO WE GO FROM HERE?

In conclusion then; the gifts of the Holy Spirit are the natural progression for a people filled with the Holy Spirit.

In Luke's gospel Jesus is filled with the Holy Spirit. *(Luke 3:22)*. He immediately understands the purpose of this baptism with the Holy Spirit as he declares His intention; He understands the purpose of the anointing of the Holy Spirit upon Him and is expecting a demonstration of the gifts of the Holy Spirit through His life. *(Luke 4:18,19)*. Every statement of His Divine Manifesto includes an expectation of healing - physical and emotional; deliverance and the miraculous.

His declaration covers most of the gifts outlined by Paul in the book of Corinthians. We concluded the last chapter with a mention of the greater works that Jesus stated believers would know. *(John 14:12)*. Jesus took the gifts of the Spirit out into the streets and into the market place. I

111

believe God is calling us to do the same, in places like Schools, theatres, Town Halls and public places as well as in our church gatherings. I believe we should be looking for words of knowledge, words of wisdom and prophetic encouragements to be released in our everyday conversation.

Our outreach adventures should be "Spirit led". I believe the "Treasure hunting" that is encouraged by Bethel Church, Redding, should be the order of the day as we expect God to reveal significant information to us in our evangelism.

Perhaps we could be used by God to write the next chapter in the book of the Acts of the Holy Spirit through a body of Spirit filled believers!

APPENDIX 1:

FURTHER THOUGHTS ON PROPHETS AND PROPHECY

This appendix is added to provide some further information to the chapter which confined itself to the gift of the Spirit; prophecy.

We start by exploring the various words used for prophecy in the scriptures.

- **Old Testament.** The Hebrew word - "Nabi" is used on several occasions and is interpreted as "spokesman or speaker". Interestingly, it is God who uses this word to describe how He will speak to Moses and then Aaron will speak for Moses. It means "One who speaks on behalf of another". *(Ex 4:14-16)*. It is clearly meant to describe the function of speaking on behalf of another. *(Ex 7:1)*.

"Chazah" is another word that is used several times. It means "a seer, one who sees, to behold." *(Amos 7:12)*. The most common word is "ra'ah" which is translated as; "to see, seer". *(1Sam 9:19)*. There is a beautiful simplicity about the word, as the prophet – sees! Often in the Old Testament God revealed prophetic truth through things that were seen.

- **New Testament.** This word is used exclusively in the New Testament. "Prophetes" is a composite word, that means it is the combination of at least 2 words. The words are "pro" which means before, or on behalf of, and "phemi" which means "to declare or say". In other words, it means "to speak on behalf of God". It also means to declare beforehand. "Psuedoprophetes", which means false prophet, is the only other word used.

Putting those words together we can draw this conclusion. It means to forthtell and to foretell, not fortune tell. Fortune telling and all other forms of predicting the future are the counterfeit. Prophecy is the real thing. I have heard people suggest that prophecy is "like fortune telling". I suggest when we speak in this way we undermine the real thing and fall into the trap of attributing the work of God to the powers of darkness. Fortune telling is the counterfeit of the real thing. Never compare prophecy with fortune telling. All forms of future telling are a counterfeit of the real thing.

Diversity of the prophetic.

There are three different and distinct ways in which we declare the prophetic. First of all in a general sense we are a prophetic people. *(1 Pet. 2:9).* All believers and churches are called to be prophetic, to communicate the Divine Will and values of the Kingdom. Every action and activity reflected by our lifestyle should be making a prophetic statement. There is a sense in which every area of our life should be a prophetic statement: in our marriages, our working life as well as our family life. The second area is the Gift of Prophecy - The inspirational exercise of the gift. *(1 Co 12:10, 14:1-3,31).* The third is the Ministry of the Prophet. This is the man or woman standing in the office of the prophet. *(Eph. 2:20, 4:11-16)*

Definition of Prophetic Ministry.

- One who speaks on behalf of God
- One to whom and through whom God speaks
- One who declares the Divine purpose of God
- One who foretells and forthtells the mind of God
- One who communicates God's will

Distinction between Prophets and Prophecy.

The Inspirational Gift is both spontaneous and unpremeditated. *(1 Co 12:10, 14:3,4).* It is often called the simple or general gift. Its parameters are to comfort, encourage and strengthen. It is spontaneous, spasmodic and limited in its content. It is not predictive or directive. This gift is able to be exercised by all believers. *(1 Co 14:31)*

The office and Ministry of the Prophet is different in that the person is the gift. They are called to this work of

Revelation. It is a divine appointment. *(Eph. 2:20, 4:11-16, 1Co 12:28)*. It is a permanent ministry; its outworking includes words of knowledge and wisdom, visions, dreams, preaching and teaching. Revelation comes through waiting upon God. It is much more than simply words of encouragement.

On occasions I have moved in the office of the Prophet and received significant prophetic words of a directional nature. I remember being in Zimbabwe at a crucial time and bringing a word which had national relevance for the church in a difficult political situation. I was awake most of the previous night as the Spirit spoke to me. The next morning, instead of my prepared message, I prophesied for 25 minutes. The word I brought was copied and sent to many churches and leaders in the nation and has been fulfilled over the last 10 years. This has not happened to me many times. I believe this example illustrates the way in which the prophet moves. I usually find I move in a simple prophetic word, which sometimes includes gifts of revelation.

Relevance of the Prophetic today.

It is stated that the evidence of an outpouring of the Holy Spirit is seen in an increase of prophetic activity. *(Mal. 4:5, Acts 2:17,18)*. Peter includes every person as he speaks of the coming of the Spirit. God is raising up Prophets and releasing prophecy. The scriptures show this is a major mark of the outpouring of the Spirit. Every barrier is coming down. The gender barrier is removed as, *"Sons and daughters" "servants both men and women"* are told they will prophesy. Any trace of ageism disappears as *"Old men and also young men"* will hear from heaven in different ways. The barrier of social status and class is irrelevant as are told, *"even on your servants"*, (word is slaves) prophecy will take place. Lack of education or our poor economic background are not barriers for experiencing the outpouring of the Holy Spirit. In reality, Charismatic history is full of stories of ordinary people who did extraordinary things enabled by the Spirit. The race issue is also dealt with as Peter declares: *"This is for you" (Acts 2:39),* to at least 14 language groups, representing, Africa, Europe, the middle-east and the far-east.

This last decade has seen a serious increase in the release of prophecy in the church. This is a sign of the outpouring of the Spirit. We are seeing the fulfilment of Moses' prayer. *(Num. 11:4-29)*

Discovering our prophetic gifting.

There are various levels of prophetic gifting. I have come up with three.

- All may prophesy. This is the gift of the Spirit. Every believer can expect to move in this level of prophecy. *(1Co 14:31)*
- A Prophetic Anointing. Those who move in revelation gifts. Those who move "at times" with a prophetic anointing, but for whom this is not their primary gift. It would also apply to those who are

in training and development and who eventually will become prophets.

- The Prophet. Those whose responsibility is to bring direction to the church, to bring the mind of God, to minister the Word of revelation to individuals. Prophets are those for whom this is their primary gift. They teach, preach, inspire and train others in the prophetic. *(Eph. 4:11-16)*

- The Challenge. We can all prophesy. We are to *"earnestly desire". (1Co 14:1)*. It is only said of this gift that we can all exercise it. The reason, I suggest, is because it embraces all the vocal gifts, and encourages and inspires us to reach for the greater gifts of knowledge and wisdom, as well as being a springboard into the dynamic of the supernatural gifts of healing, miracles and faith.

The Importance of the Prophetic word.

We have already stated it is the MAJOR mark of the outpouring of the Spirit. *(Acts 2:17,18)*. I believe the prophetic word is foundational. It is essential for life and purpose. The word most used is vision. Vision is focus, direction, purpose, reason for being. *(Pro. 29:18)*. It is rooted in revelation. Somebody said, "The difference between a good idea and a vision is its source". The source of our vision is prophetic revelation. It is very significant that the word vision is translated as revelation in the New International Version. The end of this verse in the Authorised Version declares that without vision *"the people perish" (Pro.29:18)*. As dramatic as this sounds it is not the best interpretation of the word used here. In the modern versions it is better translated as "unrestrained" or "cast off restraint" (NIV and NASB). To paraphrase the verse and give it its full meaning it would be something like this: "Where there is no prophetic word (sense of purpose or direction) people do their own thing, anarchy rules, life lacks purpose." That emphasises its importance to every individual.

We see this worked out in so many lives. In their natural lives outside of the Kingdom of God, the achievers, movers and shakers have vision, even if this is often misdirected. Those who make it are driven by sense of purpose, whether that is in the world of sport, politics or business. I met the first coach of Daley Thompson, the Olympic decathlon gold medalist. He said that at the age of 13, Daley was going nowhere, but this man inspired him with a vision of what he could be. He put into his life a sense of purpose and gave him a vision of his potential. The achievements of Daley Thompson show the power of vision. Stories such as this could be repeated over and over.

However, we are looking at the prophetic dynamic of vision. Wherever you look in the Bible you find the principle illustrated. Every significant leader and successful follower of the Lord was driven by vision, inspired by prophetic revelation, however that came to them. Abraham *(Gen 12:1-3)*,Moses *(Ex 3 and 4)*, Joshua *(Josh 1:1-9)*, Paul *(Acts 26:16-18)* and of course Jesus *(Isa 53:10,11, 50:6,7, Luke 9:51)*. Timothy, who now was leading the church at

Ephesus, had a very clear sense of the prophetic word supporting and establishing him in his ministry. I believe that our view of vision and ministry depends on the importance and value of the personal, prophetic word. *"In accordance with the prophecies previously made concerning you, that by them you may fight the good fight." (1Tim1:18) "Do not neglect the spiritual gift within you, which was bestowed on you through prophetic utterance with the laying on of hands by the presbytery." (1Tim 4:14).*

For my wife and I, the whole of our lives and ministry has been a prophetic journey. Every step of our journey, every new adventure, has been related to prophetic revelation. One illustration will be sufficient at this stage. In 1985, we as a leadership in the church, were praying about our purpose as a church, believing that God had called us to be more than a local congregation. The three full-time leaders were invited to visit Bradford and meet with Bryn Jones and some of his prophetic guys.

On the journey, I shared with the leadership team how I believed the Lord was leading me to get involved in the training and development of leaders. We were soon praying together with these brothers in Bradford. One of them laid hands on my head and said, "God has called you to teach and train young men and women. You are to set your eyes upon them, lay your hands upon them and impart your gift to them. All around the world will be those on whom you have laid your hands and imparted your gift." This was an amazing confirmation of what I was feeling.

Several weeks later, I was in a large gathering and sitting

behind a prophetic couple from the USA who were speaking at our annual Bible week. During the worship, the guy turned around, looked me in the eye and said, "God has called you to be a prophet teacher, to train young men and women for the army of God". He turned again and continued to worship. I have never doubted since that God has called me to this ministry.

It is essential that we have a sense of personal prophetic purpose for what we are doing. We also require a corporate prophetic direction for our churches. It creates faith and confidence. it provides a sense of security. It brings encouragement in difficult times. Joseph was enabled to press on through the most severe pressure to receive the fulfillment of the prophetic word over his life. *(Ps 105: 17-22).*

I would suggest there are two kinds of people and two kinds of churches; Those who are growing and developing, and those who are not growing and developing. The common mark of churches and individuals who are increasing is that they always have a sense of prophetic purpose and destiny.

The necessity of the prophetic word.

- It brings direction. We have already covered that. *(Isa 30:21, 1Tim 1:18,19, 4:14)* Timothy was empowered by the prophetic word. He fulfilled his ministry because of prophetic guidance.
- It inspires faith. Depressed, discouraged people are inspired to press on as they receive and believe the

word of the Lord. The reverse is also true, as in the case of the children of Israel; they did not believe the prophetic word and so did not experience its fulfilment. *(Heb 4:2)*.

- It demonstrates the supernatural. The power of God is revealed in the prophetic as His knowledge and wisdom are demonstrated, this proving His existence. *(Isa 46:9,10)*.

- It confirms the call and purpose of God. God declares his purpose to us. *(Isa 46:11)*. Over the years, many have suggested that I should write a book but it was not until 2 years ago that Wayne Drain visited us in the UK from the USA. He brought me a clear and distinct word that it was time to write down the things that God was saying to me. This was confirmed several months later by another leader who telephoned me to say he had been in the shower and the Lord had said to him, "Tell Peter it is time to write the book"

- It reveals God's heart. It reveals God's love and interest in the affairs of mankind. *(2Pe 1:20,21)*.

- It enables us to prepare for the future. Paul was advised and aware of what the future held and was able to prepare himself accordingly. *(Acts 11:28,29)*. On several occasions I have brought prophetic words to people of impending difficulty. It is interesting that when they experienced that time of stress they thanked me for the word that had helped them through that time.

- It brings correction. There are times when the prophetic word will warn of the danger of neglecting Bible truths.
- It challenges complacency. The prophetic word comes to stir us up, to challenge apathy and lethargy. *(Hag 1:3,4).*
- It edifies, comforts and strengthens; it encourages, exhorts and builds up. *(1Cor 14:3).*

Evaluating the prophetic word.

There are two aspects of prophecy. Firstly, the unconditional. This is when there are no conditions, caveats, or "if" and "then" words related to the prophecy. It is usually when God declares His purpose. There are very few of these words and their fulfilment is inevitable. Whatever we do, however we react, God will do what he has declared. It does not depend on us at all. *(Matt. 16:18, Joel 2:28,29).* Secondly, there is the conditional. The fulfilment is not inevitable. Unless the conditions are fulfilled, the word will not be fulfilled. Often principles have to be lived by for the word to come into being. The words "If"......then" often appear in these prophecies. The prophetic word over Joshua was, *"Every place that the sole of your foot shall tread upon, I have given that to you". (Josh. 1:3).* If Joshua had not trodden on any land but stood still, he would not have inherited the land and seen the prophecy fulfilled. If Paul had stayed in Jerusalem, no Gentiles would have been reached by the Gospel. *(Acts 26:16).*

Prophecy is usually:

- A vision of the possibilities
- A promise with a challenge

- A declaration with a condition
- An indication of your potential
- A word that demands a response

Weighing prophecy.

I would like to suggest some guidelines for deciding if a prophetic word is credible.

- Consider the messenger. Who is the person bringing the word? Do they have credibility, and what is their reputation? Jesus said, *"Therefore by their fruits you shall know them". (Matt.7:20).* By their fruits we should make judgement and evaluate people. When it comes to prophecy we want to know who they are, where are they from, their history and the proof of their ministry. I remember an occasion in Fort Lauderdale. A guy we were with complained, because he went to a church of 500 people for the first time and was not allowed to share a prophetic word with the congregation. He was not known by anyone on the congregation. In this case, my advice would be to get them to share the content of their word after the meeting, with the leadership of the church. We should look at their character and example. The qualifications for ministry relate to behaviour. Disqualification is on the basis of a person's character, not the quality of their gift or ability. *(2Tim. 2:21, 1Tim. 3:1-13).* There is also the issue of motivation and accountability. There is a danger of the prophet misusing the gift in the area of manipulation and control. This is dangerous and unacceptable. Beware of prophets without pastoral accountability. I have seen prophetic people offering words for money. I was present at a gathering, where the guy ministering offered the front row for $1000 and the second row for $500. Prophecy was offered on the ability to pay for it. This is completely unacceptable.

- Consider the message, the attitude with which it is given, *(2Tim. 2:24,25)* and also consider the Biblical content. *(Isa 8:20)*. It must be in line with the truth and values of the Word of God and the Spirit of God. It should contain correct doctrine and valid experience. A word of caution; sometimes the prophetic word contains revelation beyond the common understanding or experience of those present. The message should be Jesus centred. The message must lead us to Jesus. *(Rev 19:10)*.

- Consider the application. We must consider carefully the meaning of the revelation. We should interpret prophecy carefully and thoughtfully. It often has more than one fulfilment and application. The Bible is full of examples of this nature. *(Isa. 7:14, Acts 2:16-21)*. We should consider the matter of timing. The word over Paul about him going to the Gentiles took 13 years to come to pass. *(Acts 26:16-19, 13:1-3)*. The time between the dreams that Joseph had and their fulfilment was also around 3 years. The promise over Abraham probably took towards 50 years to be fulfilled. Many people go into a depression of doubt if the prophetic word is not completed within months. There are also sometimes implications alongside the word. Sometimes there is action that needs to take place to see a word come into being. For example, if someone was called to China, I would expect them to commence learning the language and studying the history and geography of the people.

Confirming the prophetic word.

- There is a principle in the scriptures that I have called "The Witness Principle". All the following scriptures emphasise the importance of a two-fold or even better a three-fold witness to confirm and establish truth. This must also be true for the prophetic word. *(Matt. 18:16-20, Deut. 19:15, John 18:17, 1Tim. 5:19, Heb. 10:28, 1Cor. 13:1, 1John 5:8)*

This means, that all prophetic words, should have a two-fold or three-fold confirmation. The prophetic often follows the following pattern.

- God speaks.......Personally and directly. *(Col. 3:15)*
- He confirms........Prophetically *(Rom. 8:14)*
- He establishes....... Authenticates by the Word of God or through Godly leadership. *(Ps. 119:105, Isa. 8:20, Heb. 13:17)*

Feelings can be treacherous; prophets are fallible and sometimes get it wrong. It is Jesus brings this protective principle to safeguard us. Again, for my wife and I, this has been a guiding principle that we have worked to. One evening, after 3 years pastoring our first church, I was speaking on the telephone to a brother who told me that the leader of a church in East London was unwell. As I put the phone down, I felt the Lord say to me, "You are going to this church". The Holy Spirit came upon me and I knew that it was a word from God. The next day I was with my brother, who said to me, "I was praying yesterday and felt the Lord say to me that you are going to this same church in Walthamstow". Several weeks later I was reading the scripture from Jeremiah and knew that God had put this in my heart as the verse I read established the purpose of God for our next season. It took several years to be fulfilled, but on many occasions since we have waited on this principle, until the prophetic word came to pass.

There is also the Fulfillment Principle. The prophets speak of those who have a vision of their own imagination. If a word does not come to pass, then a prophet has not spoken. *(Deut. 18:18-22, Jer. 23:16-22, Eze 13:17)* n the Old Testament false prophets were stoned to death. Perhaps if we initiated some stoning meetings, we might deal with some of the more extreme prophetic antics of some!

It is important to mention the Scripture Principle. God never speaks outside of the principles of the Bible: doctrine and experience, truth and testimony, Word and Spirit. *(Isa 8:20, John 8:32, Roms 6:17)*

Appropriating the prophetic word.

There are at least seven hindrances to the fulfillment of the Prophetic Word; barriers that will thwart and hamper the effectiveness of prophecy.

- Unrighteousness. Joshua at Ai did not possess the city that had been promised prophetically, because of sin in the camp. *(Jos. 7:1)*
- Lack of Faith. Because they did not take hold of the prophetic promise, the children of Israel spent 40

years in the wilderness. Three million people never entered the prophetic purpose of God for their lives. *(Heb. 4:2, 10:36)*

- Prayerlessness. The prophetic word does not mean we give up praying and wait. The prophetic word should encourage and inspire us to pray the word into being. We continue and increase in our spiritual disciplines. *(Jos. 7:6, 9:14, Acts. 13:2,3, 1Kings 18:41-16)*

- Lack of Perseverance. Joseph had to persevere to see the word come to pass. The lives of Paul and Abraham also illustrate this truth. *(Ps 105:17-20)*

- Passivity. The people had settled down and were enjoying the meetings instead of entering into their prophetic destiny and actively pursuing their vision. *(Jos.18:1-3)*.

- Human Interference. Abraham (with Ishmael) tried to help God out! We must wait for God to work and not try to engineer the fulfilment of the word. *(Gen. 16:1,2)*

- Unwillingness to pay the price. There is always a price to pay. Many do not enter their prophetic destiny because they are unwilling to pay the price. *(Acts 26:19-22)*.

Positive action is demanded to see the fulfillment of the prophetic word. Stake your life on it; live for it; press through to see it; die for it.

Discerning the prophetic.

The following are a number of ways the prophetic comes:

- Visions. Most visions we see in our minds and imaginations. Occasionally one might see an open vision. *(Jer. 1:11,12. Acts 2:17, Acts 10:3)*

- Dreams. Very common in the Old Testament and in Third World situations where they have no Bible. In the present day there does seem to be an increase in significant prophetic dreams. *(Num. 12:6)*[14]

- Impressions. Often a feeling of sadness or joy can be an indication of a prophetic word prompting us to vocalise a word.

- Seeing Words. There are times when you might see a Word which expresses the prophetic destiny or gifting of a person.

- Still Small Voice. The most common way of hearing the prophetic is that still, quiet, inward voice. Listening carefully! *(1 Kings 19:11-13)*

- Audible voice. God does speak audibly at times, although this is quite unusual and rare. *(1 Sam. 3.)*

- Scripture. As the Holy Spirit is the author of the Word, it is hardly surprising that he often brings a scripture to mind as a prophetic springboard. *(1 Pet. 2:20,21)*

- Sentence. Often a phrase, a sentence, or a line from a song will spark off a prophecy.

- Objects. An article of clothing, an object, a badge, something in the room can inspire a prophetic thought.

- Symbols. You may see something that is symbolic that sparks a line of prophetic ministry.

---

[14] Pentecost Then... Pentecost Now – Peter Butt.

- Names. It is remarkable how often the meaning of a person's name is a prophetic indication of their destiny. *(Isa. 43:1,45:3,4, 49:1)*
- Creative Prophecy. This kind of prophetic word is powerful and usually exercised by someone who is a prophet. Elijah prophesying rain would be an example. *(Gen 1, Eze 37, 1Kings 18:41-46)*
- Gifts of the Holy Spirit. The gifts of the Spirit, Tongues and Interpretation, Prophecy, Words of Knowledge and Wisdom and Discernment, all include a prophetic dynamic and are a springboard into the prophetic.

Prophets and Prophecy.

There is a clear distinction between Old and New Testament Prophets. The list below indicates some of those differences.

Old Testament	New Testament
To the nation	To the church
Applied old covenant	Applied new covenant
Focus on Law	Focus on Grace
Focus on Rules	Focus on church

We do not look to the Old Testament model but Jesus as the model. John the Baptist was the last in the line of Old Testament prophets.

The role of the Old Testament prophet is now carried out by the church who should be the prophetic voice to a nation. I would suggest that the Old Testament Prophet equates more to the New Testament Evangelist. His role was to call the people back to God. I am disturbed when I see people calling themselves "Prophets" and modelling themselves on the Old Testament calling. The New Testament prophet is a foundation layer and functional ministry.

In the Ministry of the New Testament Prophet, is a calling to the following work alongside the other ministry gifts. *(Eph 2;20, 4:11-16).*

- To Equip. *(Eph 4:12, Acts 13:2).*
- To Build Up. *(Eph 4:12, Acts 15:32)*
- To Bring Unity. *(Eph 4:13)*
- To Bring Maturity. *(Eph 4:13)*
- To Bring Stability. *(Eph 4:14, Acts 15:32)*
- To Exalt Jesus. *(Eph 4:15, 2:20, Rev. 19:10)*
- To Grow Church. *(Eph 4:16,2:21).*

It is imperative that prophets are joined in relationship to other ministries; alongside all the other ministries. The prophet often sees what needs to be done but does not carry the anointing to carry out the work. The Apostle is the builder, the Pastor the carer, the Evangelist the soul winner, the Teacher the instructor. His gift alongside others brings the Church to *the "full measure of the stature of Christ". (Eph.4:13).* We see an example of this in The Old Testament with David and the sons of Issachar as the prophets. It states, *"They understood the times and knew what Israel should do". (1 Chron. 12:32)*. An excellent description of the prophetic.!

We aspire to be a prophetic people who in these days speak into the lives of individuals, the church and the nation.

May God bless you as you step into your prophetic anointing.

APPENDIX 2:

PROPHETIC ASSIGNMENT

(This is the assignment we set for our Prophetic Module in our School of Ministries programme. We have been greatly inspired by those who have worked through this.

The assignment is in 2 parts:

1. Choose a family in the church who are not well known to you, and target them for prayer and prophetic encouragement. Follow the rules of the assignment as laid down by the School.

2. Write a CASE STUDY for each step you take.

We want to be able to see your progress throughout the assignment and be able to comprehend your thinking and understanding. Write a report alongside each stage of the assignment.

Choose a family in the church who are not well known to you. Seek the Lord prayerfully for a few weeks (with fasting if necessary) asking for a word of encouragement for them.

Ask God to give you His burden for them at this time. Try to make sure you are receiving His heartbeat for them.

What is God saying to you through this?

Write down Words, Pictures and any relevant Scripture, that you receive. Pray over it.

Determine what type of word it is. Is it:

- Inspirational and encouraging?
- Directional and stimulating?
- Correctional and challenging?

Explain the purpose of the Word and your choice.

Write it down and share it with the leaders of your church or the course you are completing. Allow it to be judged and weighed. Take notice of the appropriate advice from the leadership.

Wait for confirmation from your leaders that it is acceptable to share the word.

Write down the advice and counsel that your leaders gave you.

As you are given the go-ahead to deliver the word, think about how you will do that. Which method will you use?

Written Word, Symbolic act, Drama, Spoken Word, Visual object, Song.

Explain on paper the method you use and why.

Choose the time and deliver the Word. Make sure there is a leader or designated person present.

Give yourself marks out of 10 (10 being the highest mark) for your actual delivery of the prophecy.

Marks Out Of 10 Your Mark

a)   Conveying God's love and acceptance

b)   Introduction, putting people at ease

c)   Content of the prophecy

d)   Method of delivery, presentation

e)   Your own level of grace and humility

f)   Conclusion, prayer and advice

How was the prophecy recorded?

Were there clarifications required at the conclusion of delivery? If so, what explanations or clarifications did you give and why?

Thinking back, write down anything you would change or improve. Next time you do this exercise, what you would do differently?

Describe how the assignment has affected your:

- perception of prophecy and how it should be used
- working relationship with leaders
- integrity and credibility in ministry
- ability to feel and communicate God's heart to others

Hand in the whole assignment. A written copy of the Prophetic Word and your case study before the deadline given.

If you complete this assignment correctly you will have learned, how to: prepare your heart before the Lord; to listen carefully; pursue the love of God for the people you prophesied over; decide the pattern and order of the word you are receiving; understand and explain the type of prophecy you have received, and how to work with your leadership as you develop in the prophetic realm; receive advice and counsel in the shaping of the prophecy; determine the methodology you will use in delivering any future prophecy; examine honestly your practise of delivery and any adjustments you might be required to make; administrate the prophecy correctly; submit to the feedback of your leadership or mentor; understand and express how the prophetic ministry has affected you personally; exercise self-control as you move from a purely spontaneous prophetic style to a more considered, planned and disciplined prophetic approach to ministry.

Finally:

Congratulations! If you've made it this far, you'll probably feel as if you've just finished your first competitive marathon!! Hopefully you will have been stretched in mind and spirit.

Now you need to practise and add experience in order for the whole process to become habitual and Godly.

Start praying about your next prophetic adventure.

BIBLIOGRAPHY

He Still Speaks - Wayne Drain and Tom Lane. (http://www.waynedrain.com)

Developing your Prophetic Gifting - Graham Cooke

Growing in the Prophetic - Mike Bickle

User Friendly Prophecy - Larry Randolph

Prophets and Personal Prophecy - Bill Hamon

The Gift of Prophecy - Wayne Grudem

Spiritual Gifts – Aaron Linford

Seven Pentecostal Pioneers – Colin Whittaker.

ABOUT THE AUTHOR

Peter Butt trained in the Assemblies of God Bible College. Since 1970 he has been involved in church leadership. He founded and established the School of Ministries leadership training programme out of New Community Church, Southampton. He travels widely nationally and internationally training leaders as well as overseeing churches in the UK. He is married to Irene and has four married children, seven grandchildren and two great grandchildren.

If you have been inspired, challenged, confused, puzzled, or just want to discuss any of the ideas or issues raised in this book, Peter would be happy to hear from you on his personal email: peterb@newcommunity.org.uk.

Also, if you haven't already read it, take a look at Peter's first book, "Pentecost Now... Pentecost Then..." here: http://link.jascottpublications.com/pnpt

Peter is currently working on a final book in this series due in Autumn 2019 with a working title of *"Pentecost Released – A Fresh Look at Leadership in the church"*

If you would like a FREE preview of this book, or are interested in keeping up to date with Peter's book releases and teaching material, simply head on over to www.jascottpublications.com/peterbutt and find out more.

Peter will shortly be releasing a teaching series on the Baptism and the Gifts of the Holy Spirit. This will include Video Content, Teacher and Student Notes, with Presentation Slides.

Keep an eye on the website for more details.

www.jascottpublications.com/peterbutt

17360999R00081

Printed in Great Britain
by Amazon